Stamp of the Congress of the Republic of Peru.
Lima, 1828

Towards the Bicentennial: Brief Constitutional History in Peru (2018)

José Francisco Gálvez

To my family from both Hemispheres.

With sincere gratitude to the Faculty of Law of
The Pontifical Catholic University of Peru
For its centenary

1919 - 2019

Peru is our homeland and its history ours, let's begin.

SUMMARY

INTRODUCTION

Previous words

Be the first words to thank the will and work of the great friend and lawyer Alfredo Flores Chávez, who had the generosity to revise the text in the English version to make it more understandable, leaving it ready for your critical reading. A story that becomes necessary to take back then when "everything is said, but as nobody listens it is necessary to start again" (André Gide).

Every day we fulfill dates, although we do not always commemorate them, we usually go to the ephemeris in order to listen to a relevant event in the past and to think about it. It is the evolution of our nature to go to the past tense as a nostalgia, a pleasant moment or a conflictive and violent event. The fashion of the bicentennial came from the reminder of the revolutions of Western civilization as was the American (1776) and the French (1789).

Models whose influence continues to impact the generations and so continue because they not only occurred in a cause-effect relationship but were the result of an ideology that was imposed progressively and proclaims rights that would take to be universally reassessed until the twentieth century. Peru, land hungry for discoveries, never ceases to amaze the most rational inhabitant of the planet for its resources as its people. To emulate other democratic systems is praiseworthy, but let's not forget its idiosyncrasy without which, the way citizen participation is exercised would be catastrophic. It is better to admit what we are to achieve an institutional reflection in accordance with the reality that regulates us. The bicentennial allows us to maintain that Peruvian democracy has been and is a dynamic system, assisted not only by its Constitution and laws, but also by incipient facts and ethics related to informality in all aspects that are close to governance. from the country.

Proximity to the year 2021 gives us the time to show that informality persists, at considerable levels and whose existence, rather than being combated by the State, must have a measurement by parameters or indicators, rather than the superficial application of a norm. condice with the spirit of regulation itself. Hence, our title: Of the fact the right is born, an affirmation that implies looking in our culture for the elements that are abstracted and then elevating their understanding of the daily level to the academic. The role of the State, whose presence is far away in the inhospitable areas, giving rise to little or no control over it as an authority, forgetting that it can delegate, but under constant supervision, its functions in entities of society.

Peru is far from being a monolithic state, becoming even informal in the actions of its authorities, especially policies. A current but not new fact has been and is corruption. He resided in the governing authorities of the king, although it was called abuse and for that reason the residence trial was established, in order to know how the monarch's resources had been used. Judgment that continued during the Republic. Replaced in 1867 by a technical process that included the high state officials, it was thought that the bad practice of a few could not leave in question the entire system.

At present, this phenomenon has overflowed and includes the top managers of national and foreign companies. Only exemplary measures, without any benefit for the offender, can regain the trust of society in the State. Circumstance that also requires adjustments in constitutional matters, whose content is part of the daily rules of the society. The bicentennial represents the propitious occasion to know how much we have advanced in the satisfaction of our needs, totally or partially, and to become more involved in our development, conquering Peru for the Peruvians, but not forgetting the hospitality that has characterized us for all cosmopolitan.

The constitutional history marks and course that invites us to reflect on the facts and how we have narrated them. Marco Tulio Cicero in his work Speaking dialogues maintained: History itself, witness of the times, light of truth, life of memory, teacher of life, messenger of antiquity, ¿with what voice speaks to immortality but with the voice of the speaker?

This discipline has always represented an obligatory resource to delve into the analysis of the past in order to understand the current evolution of our institutions. Reasoning in which the present version of the constitutional history is framed that recreates not only contributions of the important documents such as Letters, statutes, decrees or constitutional laws but the previous or subsequent events, as well as the current thought that made them an instrument of innovation of the established order, strengthening or undermining the current organizational model. In that sense, we analyze from a historical perspective the constitutional scope through an interdisciplinary framework (cultural, political and legal), focusing on whether it responds to patterns of rupture or continuity in the book's temporal arc. Explanation that does not intend to exhaust it with its narrative but to raise reflections of the author on the circumstances occurred and embodied in the relevant chapters. Through the following chapters I go to two parameters that can be very useful to know the development of the policy. The cultural and the political, which have acted according to the concept of State that has been varying until arriving at the Constitutional Democratic nature.

Cultural because the design of a society has never been alien to the idiosyncrasy of its inhabitants, imposed or consensual, held by power groups, dynastic or not, belonging to some guild or emerging groups where society assigned a role as the notable of the nineteenth and twentieth centuries to which are added the current media leaders arising in belligerent circumstances against the authority and who then want to become themselves, known as contentious representatives (Panfichi, 2010).

Circumstance proposed by our first question. On what lies the legitimacy of political models and government regimes? Are they fickle because of the character of the inhabitants? Aristotle in Politics had pointed out, three centuries before Christ, that under that character the society contemplated two types of authorities, the legitimate one that responded to the current system of designation and illegitimate, the one that, although usurping power, ended up being accepted and therefore legitimated. In that democracy, it was in the assembly of the city or polis, where the energy of the leader who shared the common interest of the city, as Euripides stressed in the year 420 BC, was glimpsed:

"When laws are written, both the poor and the rich have equal justice. The weak can answer the powerful with the same words if he insults him; The lower one overcomes the superior if he has justice at his side. Freedom consists in this phrase: Who has a useful advice to give to the city (polis) and want to make it known? "

Peruvian viceroyalty was no stranger to demands from different sectors since the sixteenth century, accompanied by rebellions and uprisings against the actions of those who represented the Spanish crown. Claims that articulated different petitions being the indigenous the most recurrent with the abolition of mita. That not only was known in America but even for Spain itself. Fray Calixto of San José Túpac Inca gave the monarch in his own hand around 1750 the memorial: Real representation and exclamation surrendered and regrettable that the entire Indiana Nation makes the Majesty of the King of Spain and Emperor of the Indies Lord Don Fernando VI. Mita that the Liberator Jose de San Martin removed in 1821 and then will be returned during the Bolivarian administration, and finally abolished by decision of the Libertador Ramon Castilla in 1854.

The protests also served to measure the strength of the networks of communal authorities or curacas against mayors, mayors and viceroys, the perception by the questioning of the increase in customs duties, access to the jobs of the Indian bureaucracy that benefited the the European Spaniards, the loss of profits of the guilds settled in New Spain or Mexico and New Castile or Peru with the creation of viceroyalties and general captaincies. The implementation of the eighteenth-century measures known as the Bourbon reforms would not cease with the political break with Spain as they continued during the republican period, under the same liberal Catholic thought only that rooted in the mentality of the Peruvian rulers of the nineteenth century. Reflections that he raised in the first chapter where I resort to two brilliant thinkers: José Baquíjano y Carrillo and Juan Pablo Viscardo y Guzmán to continue with the prelude to Peruvian independence. Later, the founding act of the Peruvian State and culminate with the convocation of the Constituent Congress of 1822.

The difficulty in recreating a political model, as argued by François Xavier Guerra (1996), became the constant concern of thinkers and politicians, who had to link their Western theory with the confused media and long-term panorama of the American continent. For this reason, it was important to determine, in HogngAthenian usage, useful advice, based on a common history as a hallmark of our identity or its need to create it. Concern that refers us to the vision of the power group that reconstructs the past as it was or how it should be to justify its present and future acts, even more so when the State that is born is confessional until 1979.

Historical process that, on the other hand, has demonstrated the survival of current elements and that gives this discipline action over time. From this continuity comes the tradition, described by some as an obstacle to progressive progress, when in fact it contains principles and qualities conceived under moral guidelines developed by the people throughout their existence.

The second chapter begins with the first congress and goes until the end of the 1830s in the political project called the Bolivian Confederation of Peru. In this period, we notice how the political and the cultural are conjugated, under whose thought the lands of curacazgo by Simón Bolívar are abolished. Later on, the interest of uniting High with Lower Peru remains, but it falls into distortions of the political communities led by caudillos whose nationalism reigns in order. Hence the internal struggles, which leads us to think if they were necessary because of the weakness of the current system, which even though it had a Constitution, the legacy had not reached the whole country.

The third chapter begins with nationalism within a period of bonanza, as was the guano resource, but also stability that will allow Peru to have a leadership in South America. Period that will have two constitutions, one more advanced than the other. Where revolutionary liberalism is replaced by the doctrinaire, which will allow a government of twelve years in two periods led by General Ramón Castilla. Moment in which the intellectuals take a position in favor of Bartolomé Herrera and others to Domingo Elías, but above all to José Gálvez Egúsquiza, his renowned leader. We contemplate the emersion of the intermediate powers or real forces, coming from society (landowners, merchants, miners, sectors of the army and intellectuals) that supported the coup or de facto regime.

Politically, new institutions are adopted from a parliamentary system of which the Presidency of the Council of Ministers was its reflection. The existence of the necessary leader or charismatic leader would end up being indispensable in the political system. The first militarism, from 1821 will be the obligatory reference until the arrival of the first president of the Republic elected by the voters: Manuel Pardo and Lavalle. The second, then, of the signing of the Treaty of Ancon that ended the War of the Pacific with Chile with the government of the National Restoration under General Miguel Iglesias del Pino.

The fourth chapter begins with the government of Nicolás de Piérola and Villena that put an end to the government of General Andrés Avelino Cáceres Dorregaray. The bipartisanship composed of the Civil Party and the Democrat. Later the coup d'etat of Augusto B. Leguía and the establishment of his New Homeland, consolidated in the Charter of 1920. Then the arrival of the third militarism, initiated with the commander Luis M. Sánchez Cerro and the expedition of the Constitution of 1933 to stop with the Government of the Military Junta of 1962. The fifth and last chapter begins with the Revolutionary Government of the Armed Forces, its reform measures, by Juan Velasco Alvarado, in the first phase from 1968 to 1975 and Francisco Morales Bermúdez Cerrutti, from 1975 to 1980. In this interim, the 1979 Constitution will express the structural reforms that have taken place, but also the innovations in politics, law and culture, which began when Quechua was declared as the official language in 1975

Our journey continues to experience a Constitutional Democratic State in a country that recovered the institutional exercise. He had to face hyperinflation and terrorism and the weakness of the system. New nuances of caudillos like Alan García Pérez and Alberto Fujimori Fujimori appear, which strengthens or weakens the institutions at the moment of being a government, through democratic means. Probably eager to preserve their share of power, leaving aside the purpose of the policy itself or principlist proposal, substituting the general interest or useful advice for the media aspect and that may end in their individual benefit. Lines that end with the current post-Constitution panorama.

Every so often, mostly in the vicinity of general elections, a sector of the population demanded the approval of a new Constitution, under the belief that this alone would change the situation of the inhabitants, especially the economy. History teaches us that this has been and is a fallacy. That life can only be made in common if each one assumes and submits to the same rules, previously stipulated, safeguarding the defense of the rights of the people. In this sense, it is just any repression that goes against the acts perpetrated against them, within reasonable and transparent mechanisms.

To this version of Towards the bicentennial: the Constitutional History in Peru that we put before you, publications such as Constitutional History go back to the year of 1852 when Dr. José Victorino Lastarria Santander (Rancagua, 1817), exiled in Lima, wrote the passages of the European crisis from the hegemony of Napoleon Bonaparte to arrive at the intersperses of the campaigns of the liberating army in the south to conclude with the government of José de la Riva-Agüero and José Bernardo Torre Tagle, first and second president of the Republic of Peru.

Later, the edition of Constitutional Questions in The Herald of Lima in 1854 written by Toribio Pacheco (Arequipa, 1828), analyzed the first republican documents issued during the San Martin administration until the 1839 Constitution. In third place, the History of the Republic of the Peru, monumental work, by Jorge Basadre Grohmann (Tacna 1903), who reconstructed institutional life under an integrating perspective of our republican life. We must add the History of the National Constitutions of José Pareja Paz Soldán (Lima, 1913) that begins with the Constitution of 1823 and ends with that of 1933. The political and constitutional evolution of Peru independent of Lizardo Alzamora Silva (Lima, 1900), reflections on our tradition in three segments corresponding to the same number of conferences.

The Peruvian constitutionalism and its problems of Domingo García Belaunde (Lima, 1944), published in the Academic Program of Law of the Pontifical Catholic University of Peru in 1970, which includes the contextual analysis within the political vicissitudes of each republican period and concludes with reference to the Constitution of 1933. History of the Republic of Enrique

Chirinos Soto (Arequipa, 1930), who incorporates into the constitutional explanation the latest facts of the viceregal administration within the European context led by Napoleon Bonaparte to culminate with the convocation to the Assembly Constituent in October 1977. Then, the work of Margarita Guerra Martinière (Lima, 1937) General History of Peru, Volume VIII, which outlines the interpersonal aspects of political, social and political life from 1827 to the end of the 20th century, finally, articles by César Landa Arroyo (Lima, 1958). The process of contemporary formation of the Peruvian State (1989) and the constitutional evolution of Peru (2002).

Towards the Bicentennial: Brief Constitutional History in Peru that we offer to the reader today reflects the work of thinkers and ideologues and their context, who raised their conception of the State, which represented in Aristotelian terms the quantity versus the quality or the fair mean of François Guizot.

I would like to thank the hospitality of my brothers Bertha and Caesar, present in the other hemisphere, which allowed my family to conclude this story.
A special recognition to Cecilia and Paloma for their perseverance.

CHAPTER ONE

The dawn of constitutionalism

I. THE INFLUENCE OF LIBERALISM AND EMANCIPATION

The presence of liberalism as an ideology and thought goes back to Europe towards the end of the 17th century, when the thinker René Descartes with his famous phrase: I think, therefore I exist; It laid the foundations for an anthropocentric vision in response to the Western political, religious and legal tradition of that time. This was guided by the Crown, the church and the nobles, actors who held the set of rights or privileges. With this a rationalism was introduced that progressively questioned the system, built on a series of faculties and obligations between the monarch and the subjects, supervised by the Canon Law, which had printed since centuries ago a way of thinking and acting with a high ingredient axiological Faced with the discretion and decision of the authority, as magistrates and administrators, the variety of norms was subordinated, which were not always respected, giving rise to arbitrariness or excess of power and the consequent protests of sectors of the population that cried for the dismissal of the abuses.

The stability of the regime, which until then had been realized by pacts, and the mediatic circumstances in each kingdom, gradually favored the political concentration around the monarch, first in England, then in France and Spain. Stage known as absolutism and later called as Illustrated Despotism, which encumbed the king as the sun, because everything revolved around him. Even the church, had to submit to his designs. Process in which, rationalism managed to substitute in the thought of academics the theocentric vision for that one where the man, by means of his method and doubt, refined his reasoning in the search of the truth; which also led to a change in the exercise of power. The king acted for the people, but without him. He acted according to what he believed was right and good; without questioning An absolutism that provided a stony image by strengthening centralism and administration, promoting scientific development within the program of reforms that would provide welfare to the population. Added to this, the acceptance of the proposal of the enlightened to spread through education this eagerness for knowledge, based on reason. Criteria that would be put to the test in times of crisis and that ended up being invoked to evaluate the corrective measures of the crown, implicitly questioning the authority. Faced with possible reprisals, the enlightened themselves and within them the encyclopaedists, divulged the need to protect the detractors under the logic that there were "natural laws" or inherent rights to the person summarized in freedom, property and security and that they were beyond the monarch's discretion. The facts raised, first in England with the pressure of a sector of the House of Commons led by Oliver Cromwell against the arbitrary decisions of the Catholic King Charles I, who inherited the absolute power of his predecessors; they marked a change in the political leadership at the end of the tense relationship between the legislative branch and the executive branch with the real beheading, a century before the French. Fact that since then laid the foundations for the constitutional monarchy and power in that State, in charge of the nobility, lasting until the twentieth century.

The eighteenth-century French episode was characterized by the absolute power of King Louis XVI with the collaboration of the court nobility. During its mandate, the precarious economy evidenced the distorted management of public finances by the wars, which, added to the little income of the State due to the decrease of harvests and famine, demanded more pressure on the population. The social discontent echoed the messages of the enlightened mentality that argued that a cultured society could limit the regime, elements that caused a further protest to unleash in the French Revolution. Faced with the crisis, the monarch convened the States General, medieval assembly composed of the nobility, the church and the third state-the bourgeois people, whose vote was so far by estamento. Which was questioned by the bourgeois deputies, claiming that it was per capita, also getting members of the clergy and two nobles to join their ranks. Fact that caused the king to prohibit their entry into the legislative area, then decided to meet to form the national assembly, attributing the representation of the people of France, which remained to write and approve the Constitution, which would call constituent assembly and more forward convention. Terms that ceased to be factual to be incorporated into the intellectual baggage called constitutional and of which the Peruvian constitutional tradition used in its political journey. Subsequent events reaffirmed the strength of this legislature, encouraging his majesty to invite nobles and members of the clergy to conform it. Collegiate who would approve the Declaration of Rights of Man and Citizen (1789) and the French Constitution of 1791, constitutional monarchy. With this we contemplate the alteration of the bases of the absolutist regime, which lost control of the reformist measures under the ideological discourse of the bourgeoisie, which managed to capture more spaces of power with the support of the majority sectors.

Since the government of Felipe V, Duke D'Anjou and first Bourbon to occupy the throne, Enlightened Despotism established a set of measures known as the Bourbons that sought to clean up the Spanish economy at the expense of overseas raw materials, after the war of Succession. This required knowledge of the political, social and economic status, as well as the collection of scientific and cultural information that would provide a comprehensive view of the contributions of the New World to the metropolis.

The decree of dissolution of privileges (1707) imposed the theory of regalism or statism based on the inalienable rights or royalties held by the king, which the Habsburg dynasty had shared with the nobility and church, unless the privileges were consented for your highness. Rights that covered quotas and functions of power referred to jurisdictional function, the sale of public positions or venality of the offices, as well as the claim based on the principle of obedience to inapplicable a rule. Practices that had been developed in Spanish law and then in the Indian in the case system or casuisme.

The Bourbons, who embodied the State, endeavored to establish a unitary national regime, pillar of the new political legal structure, ruling as a protective father for the welfare of their children but without consulting them, basing their actions on the laws of nature. In this way the political leadership depended on royalty to the detriment of the Courts. The Councils of the kingdoms ceased to be such to form one of a national nature and henceforth would be called of its Majesty, which was composed of senior stable officials called ministers, devoted to the knowledge of different offices of the centralized administration for all the empire, with which the regional identification was eliminated.

The orders of the authority were based on the man-dato-obedience principle, being accepted by the vassal without questioning since the crown sustained it in its divine origin. Although it predates its existence, the pactist or consensus government model allowed to claim under a diffused power by which an unjust measure was resorted to at the discretion of the authority, which demonstrated flexibility or tolerance in some cases.

II. LIBERALISM IN AMERICA

In America, the Creoles recreated this principle of mandate-obedience in the continent, where real power, as is known, was indirectly maintained. Added to this was the validity of Indian standards with the Castilian women who enjoyed flexibility in their compliance with the obedience, but did not comply, through the diffused power mentioned. But the insistence of the Bourbon reforms in the eighteenth century, provoked a progressive rejection by invoking the rectification of the rigid measures, which were taking various edges as they were accentuating. The illustration, by proposing innovations transformed the nature of the monarchy and made it possible for the subjects or vassals to become compatriots or fellow citizens, in whose reasoning the phrase: Long live the King, the bad government dies; It did not rule out the legitimate ownership of power or its origin, but a vindication of peoples with different languages and cultures in front of the Spanish nation.

Meanwhile in the Peruvian viceroyalty the different social forces were preserved: the nobles, the religious, the professionals, the merchants, the peasants, as well as the institutions: the city, the fief, the abbey or the cathedral. Even when it was presumed that each one played a role in this society, equality as rights was between their peers or similar, being based on their respective corporation, according to the Hispanic model.

With the advent of Enlightenment in America, concern was raised to rediscover reality as a phenomenon that not only led to the political sphere, but also to the cultural goal of deepening the search for happiness through the model of progress Western culture within a paternalistic vision of the king that would lead to a more harmonious and balanced world. Thus, nature regained its leading role in the scientific scene, led hand in hand with history, in whose relationship we find tradition and innovation.

The crown maintained the diffusion of the ideas of the Enlightenment as long as it was not incompatible with the political system. Hence, the need to prohibit the circulation of works, since the mid-eighteenth century, especially those that influenced the postponed claim of Creole or American intellectuals, who, although they represented a minority, claimed the equality of opportunity of his Spanish peers. The regime opted to promote research and knowledge. Sociedad Amantes del País was created with the aim of delving into the description of the territory and the history referred to the territory of which they were a part, with the purpose of bringing the reader closer to a recreated cultural vision that supported the crown. In this way, the illustrated reader reflected on his identity. The Peruvian Mercury or the political, ecclesiastical and military guide of the viceroyalty of Peru for the year 1793 of José Hipólito Unanue and Pavón are an example of this relationship between politics and education.

The interest for a better Caroline administration led to the establishment of new administrative divisions within the Indian or American communities, which kept the king as lord or head. With this eagerness, the Bourbon program made evident the imposition of the intendancies, first in Spain (1711), then in Buenos Aires (1782) and finally in Peru (1784). At the same time there was the creation of the viceroyalties of Nueva Granada or Santa Fe de Bogotá and that of Buenos Aires that dismembered the Peruvian because in the first the territory of Maynas was moved and in the second, Puno. Reforms that in the end were propitiated within the Spanish empire and therefore were not - to the Hispanic legal tradition, hence they preserved much of the way the Habsburgs proceeded: The only thing that varies are the needs and talents but not the structures (Pérez-Prendes 1988, p.316).

Measures that were complemented with a new conception of law from power. Carlos III gradually imposed the criterion that those who criticized government acts committed crime, not because they questioned the acts themselves but because the distrust between the subjects was broken. Budget that prevented the control of power with the establishment of the imposed and coercive law.

The political opinion of intellectuals of the time was not exempt from these events. It is in it that we can sketch the first pre-constitutional texts: The Eulogy to His Excellency Mr. Agustín de Jáuregui and Aldecoa, Knight of the Order of Santiago, Lieutenant General of the Armies, Viceroy, Governor and Captain General of the Kings of Peru, Chile, etc. .; pronounced by José Baquíjano y Carrillo, from Lima, professor of Vespers of Laws since 1780; who openly criticized the prevailing system for the sake of its reform, after the Rebellion of Túpac Amaru.

The Letter to the Spanish Americans, originally from an anonymous author, written by the ex-Jesuit Juan Pablo Viscardo y Guzmán, pampacolquino, who opted for emancipation, after the order of the Society of Jesus was expelled from all the Spanish-American territory.

In the eulogy that until then was the speech of reception of the new viceroy to the City of Kings, Baquíjano y Carrillo gave it a reflective reformist nuance by narrating the experience of Jauregui and Aldecoa in Chile as Captain General, as well as the movements generated in Peru for the Bourbon measures, thus departing from the routine protocol. In effect, the environment of the viceroyalty had convulsed with such measures in favor of the crown, but to the economic, administrative and social detriment of the members of the community, determining the increase in protests where participation did not differentiate the race from social actors and politicians, counting on the participation of Spaniards, Creoles, mestizos, blacks and Indians, the most significant being that of Túpac Amaru, at that time who claimed for the mita and the abuse of the Corregidor de Indios.

In fact, the success or failure of the Bourbon reforms was conditioned to the suitability of the bureaucrats, which in most cases translated into a policy of repression in the face of any demand, probably because of the interest of these representatives in ascending. Elogio does not cease to exhort the monarch to seek happiness by granting the citizen the propitious environment -respectable and precious- for the enjoyment of his rights. Tendency that did not depart from the approach of the Spirit of the Laws (1748) of Charles de Secondat, Baron de Montesquieu, quoted in the text, and that reproduced the demand for the recognition and validity of natural rights and whose non-observance could be controversial to the own authority.

.. that every century has its chimeras and illusions, scorned by time and that this brilliant light has convinced that improving man against his will has always been the deceitful pretext of tyranny, that the people are a spring, that forced more than he suffers his elasticity, bursts destroying the oppressive hand that oppresses and holds him (Baquíjano 1930, 518)

The act of welcome to the viceroy Jáuregui was disastrous for Baquíjano, who was sanctioned with the postponement of his promotion as oidor for more than fifteen years and the copies of the Elogio were commanded by Royal Decree of 1784. Actions that did not diminish his intellectual development and in the exercise of their academic and judicial tasks. His critical position would echo later in the arguments of the speeches of the General and Extraordinary Courts of Cádiz, where the Americans claimed equality of conditions with the European Spaniards, invoking that the Indies had joined the Crown of Castile, like other kingdoms.

The Letter to the Spanish Americans or the new political pact of Juan Pablo Viscardo y Guzmán reflects the speech of protest after the expulsion of the Jesuit order from the Hispanic territories. It recreates the conditions in which the companies of discovery and conquest took place, from the beginning and how they have gradually led to a distancing from the political system, creating an emancipatory position among its inhabitants.

The Letter posed two sequences: one historical and one doctrinal, based on the great success of the incorporation of America or the New World into universal history. After three hundred years, Viscardo y Guzmán raises reflections on the meaning and the future in the way of how this company was carried out, Criticisms that are explained by the discomfort of the ex-Jesuit, because in America in the first place the Indian legislation did grant protection both peninsular and criollo within the structure of the estate and, secondly, the casuistic system guarded by the various authorities was not entirely tax, since arbitration was fundamental to understanding the legal system, consisting of a set of privileges, before absolutism. Criticism that earned Viscardo to resume the bases of pactism from two angles: Freedom and the creation of an American identity. The validity of freedom was revealed through political events both in Spain and in America, distinguishing the levels of command and authority that existed in the political and civil society. As the state of nature came to the social coexistence, which recreated the complex political landscape of which Viscardo showed differences in the dichotomy of the nation: European Spanish and American or American Spanish.

It was necessary to reformulate the empathy of rights with the legitimacy of authority, because if we assume that those are above it, and even more so when the ownership of power comes from ourselves, then we have managed to overcome our other interests to make representation the way to carry forward the concerns of society:

Brothers and compatriots ... The discovery of such a large part of the earth is and always will be, for the human race, the most memorable event of its annals. More for us who are its inhabitants, and for our descendants, it is an object of the greatest importance (Viscardo, 1959, 19)

The measures developed by the Bourbons restricted jobs in favor to serve the crown, providing them to European Spaniards. A quick glance reveals to us that all the viceroys, half of the members of the House and that the governors, in their majority were Spanish. In this sense, Viscardo raised his voice of protest by pointing out:

... only we are considered unworthy and incapable of assuming these positions, which by the most rigorous right belong exclusively to our country (Viscardo, 1959, 208).

Gradually the argument of the Creoles in the recuperation of the public space was born, invoking the birth in the territory, based on the Roman principle of the ius soli, thus creating the American continental identity. Discrepant basis to the monarchy that argued that the effectiveness of the bureaucrats was based on no link with the place where he performed, maintaining its neutrality against social behavior and thus avoiding any type of rlationship that could affect their work.

III. THE IMPACT OF THE FRENCH REVOLUTION AND THE COURTS OF CADIZ

The legacy of the French Revolution in the New World was fundamental in most of the Creole intellectuals, because of the vindicating character in front of the power, constituting a trigger for the processes of change and that allowed to test the existing political theories, maintaining or not the current form of government. Moreover, when the Declaration of Man and Citizen was issued setting the precedent that the rights were declared and recognized without the need to invoke the status to claim them, which precipitated as the level of political tension was sharpened and before the popular pressure that It invoked the staunch defense of freedom and equality that ended in excesses. Episode that teaches us that the constitutional model has not been oblivious to irruptions that after concluded motivated the political writers to raise the incipient concept of modern State associated with the existence of the Constitution, as an incontrastable and political document.

The notion of equality became the mechanism that facilitated the emergence of sectors that sought a more equitable income under the leadership of the bourgeoisie, but then expanded to other sectors. The declaration, in its article 3, modified the axis of power, previously imposed by a representative one settled in the town or nation, whose profile was in the individual literate, owner and with an economic solvency, belonging to a community: The principle of all sovereignty resides essentially in the nation, no corporation, no individual can exercise any authority that does not emanate from it.

Thus, this notion of sovereignty upset the divinity in the legitimation of the power that had ratified the designations of its ownership, until then. The revolution, in accordance with the social contract, imposed the figure of the king as the first public official since there was no superior in France to that of the law: the king only reigns for it, and only in the name of the law can he demand obedience.

With the notion of the Rule of Law of the French, the adopted political form and power were subject to laws with the aim of protecting the individual rights of the person. These norms were conceived in an impersonal, objective and general way, said colloquially: without a proper name. Its influence irradiated in the theory of separation of powers, that provided new scopes in the political or constitutional right when offering a specialization and control of weights and counterbalances above all between the government and the national assembly or Gallic constituent, in function of the established political leadership. No one can deny that since 1789 the political society that emerged was the imperfect embodiment of an ideal. The same notion that gave rise to the state of society, as John Locke pointed out, allowed the people, in case they do not respect the rules, to regain power and go against the ruler: The right of insurrection.

The North American revolution, for its part, did not aim for social equality and formed a pluralist structure with the agreement of the representatives of the British colonies who agreed to fight their authorities. The battles produced expressed the struggle for rights before the British Parliament without being triggered by ideological fanaticism (as happened in France). Thus, their practical sense facilitated a common project of State, which did not exclude the contribution of Western European constitutionalism, which marked the guidelines with the concepts of popular sovereignty, nationality and individuality of liberalism.

The legal system, based on English Law, was not based solely on the legalist but retained the precedent principle, adapted to a federal republican regime and where the judiciary has been respected both in its judgments and in the work of its members. The liberalism that adopted different positions in the institutional sphere and that, in Spain, as in America was religious, allowed to conserve, as the struggles dissipated and the institutionality was recovered, its transcendental role in the establishment of the new political spaces.

The movements of the Americans who were clamoring for their rights would soon be transferred to the very zenith of the Spanish monarchy. The desire for French expansionism in Europe soon moved to the Motherland. In 1808, Napoleon Bonaparte convinced Manuel Godoy to influence King Charles IV and allow the Gallic army to cross the Spanish territory and capture Queen Maria and the Prince Regent Juan, allies of England; in exchange for which Carlos received possessions from that nation. The Lusitanian court moved to Brazil. Without presaging and being the troops in the peninsula, Napoleón Bonaparte pessured the king of Spain to abdicate in favor of its first-born Fernando VII and this one give the power to him, yielding it soon to his brother Jose, who from then on would adopt the name of José I.

The vacuum of power reverberated in the Iberian Peninsula but not in America. The captive Fernando VII sued the nobility and Hispanic society to act in his name and representation what provided continuity to the exercise of power, constituting a board of government. Act that was covered in the Games of Alfonso the Wise: ... when the common good was at risk, the nobles, prelates, men of fortune and good and honest people could form together in the absence of the monarch. (Second Part, title 15, law 3, 1260).

However, the situation was of such magnitude that the single commission was sufficient to cover the power vacuum. Hence, the Central Board chose to convene the Courts from May 22, 1809, which was made in medieval style by estates (nobility, clergy and corporations) being replaced by an organization of only one Chamber, with the participation of overseas domains.

Here is the first feature of constitutionalism in America, considering the notion of representative sovereignty at the continental level and under the design of the Hispanic nation. It was the first Peruvian experience, although being part of the Spanish State, within an election process organized by the church that took as its center the parishes, which had the demographic summary of each town.

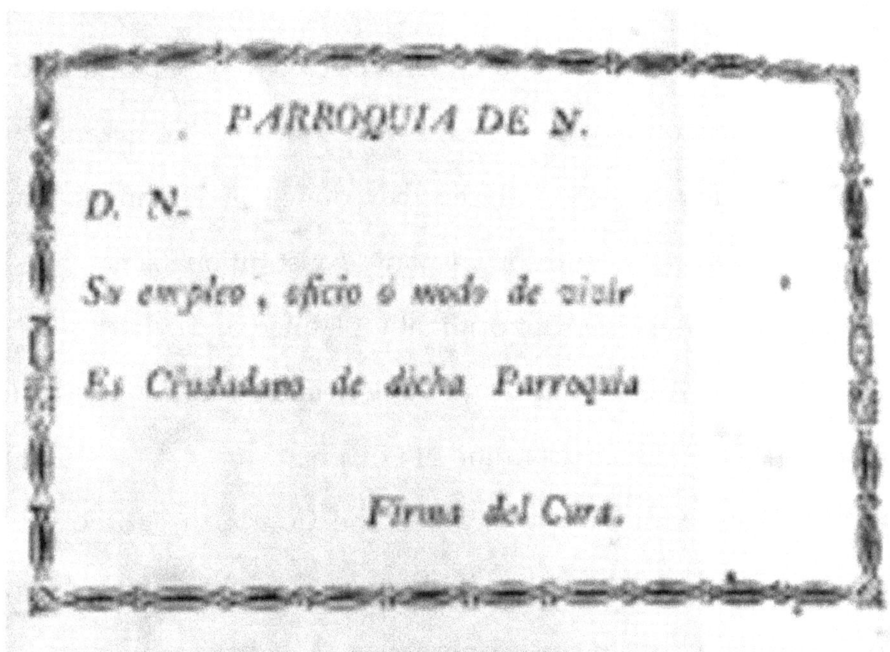

PARROQUIA DE N.

D. N.

Su empleo, oficio ó modo de vivir

Es Ciudadano de dicha Parroquia

Firma del Cura.

Parish voting card for representatives to Cádiz (1813)

Model that continued until the mid-nineteenth century. As the Courts were constituted with alternate and elected members until in each circumscription of the elections or designations, standards such as Decree I of September 24, 1810, were issued:

The deputies that make up this Congress, and that represent the Spanish Nation, are legitimately constituted in General and Extraordinary Courts, and that national sovereignty resides in them ... they recognize, proclaim and swear again by their only and legitimate King to Mr. D. Fernando VII de Borbón ... declare the General and Extraordinary Courts that reserve the exercise of the legislative power in all its extension (Cortes Generales, 1987, pp. 27-28).

Declaration that established the design of the trilogy of the exercise of power and where the Courts, on behalf of the Spanish Nation of both hemispheres, adopted the political leadership in front of the Executive Power -transitory and exercised by the Regency Council- and the Judicial Power, conformed by the Courts. Situation that is corroborated with Decree II, of September 25, when it is indicated that the Courts will receive the treatment of Your Majesty and while the captivity of Ferdinand VII lasts, the council of Highness. These decrees would show a second feature of Hispanic constitutionalism when initiating a constituent process that was not originally planned and whose pillar was based on the recreation of the concept of nation and on the other hand in what Bartolomé Clavero calls a declaration of powers.

The condition of extraordinary granted the Courts the authority to elect its rotating Presidency, without the interference of any power, having its own control body under the Powers Commission. As Clavero suggests, the proposal to draft a Constitution by the Cortes' representation was not entirely clear at the beginning, as the proposal for reforms did not imply the drafting of a fundamental Charter, more in keeping with the committees, including the one of Constitution, there is a gradual shift from the concept of mandate to representation with constituent power, thus generating "the right to establish its fundamental laws and to adopt the most convenient form of government, government in the then State sense. (Clavero, 2003, p.19).

As Marie-Danielle Demélas indicates, the quotas for the election of deputies were established on the basis of one for each:
25 thousand inhabitants (Puerto Rico), 150 thousand inhabitants (Cuba and Florida), 200 thousand inhabitants (Chile), 225 thousand inhabitants (Guatemala and Quito), 400 thousand inhabitants (Caracas), 525 thousand inhabitants (Buenos Aires), 650 thousand inhabitants (Lima), 725 thousand inhabitants (Santa Fe), 891 thousand 666 inhabitants (New Spain) and one million 200 thousand inhabitants (Philippines) (Démelas, 1992, p. 150, note 155).

Finally, the number of deputies in Cádiz was 303 representatives, although they were never all reunited due to the very circumstances of their prolonged duration.
It must be remembered that they lasted about three years during this period 1810 sessions were held, of which 978 ordinary, 18 extraordinary and 814 secret. Participating American deputies, 63 of whom ten out of a total of 37 presidents, 12 of 35 vice presidents and 11 of 36 secretaries (Meléndez, 1987, p.111).
The Creoles in their proposal of the Peruvian Deputies to the Cortes of Cadiz on the equality of peninsulares and criollos, argued in article 8 that:
The Americans, Spaniards as well as Indians and the children of both classes, have the same option as the European States for all kinds of jobs and destinies, whether in the Court or anywhere else in the Monarchy, whether they are ecclesiastical, political or military (Pareja, 1951, p. 402).

Approach that will continue in parliamentary debates even more when it came to those places with high Indigenous population indexes such as Mexico, Guatemala and Peru, pockets of insurrection and where the constituents only chose to grant the treatment of legal equality.

Of the group of Americans, were representatives of the Viceroyalty of Peru: Dionisio Inca Yupanqui, deputy for Peru.- Antonio Zuazo, deputy for Peru.- José Lorenzo Bermúdez, deputy for the province of Tarma of Peru.- Pedro García Coronel, deputy by Truxillo of Peru.- Ramón Feliu, Deputy for Peru.- Vicente Morales Duárez, deputy for Peru.- José Joaquín de Olmedo, deputy for Guayaquil.- Blas Ostolaza, deputy for the King of Peru.- José Antonio Navarrete, deputy for Peru, secretary (García Belaunde, 2016, p. 96).

The situation was relevant to rethink the conditions of identity, under the auspices of a single nation, as stated by deputy substitute Ramón Olaguer Feliu (1820), born in Santiago de Chile. Based on the role of the Creoles in the Indian society, he argued that sovereignty was a function of the exercise of corresponding representation:

... America can no longer be considered as a nation stuck and subject to the peninsula but forming with it the same and only nation, the same and only family (p.2).

Argument opposed to that of the peninsular minister Joaquín de Campillo y Cossío, who pointed out that Spain was the main thing and secondary America. The new notion of sovereignty moved away from the figure of the monarch to derive to the peoples, which in Feliu's words, gave consistency to the sum of the parts, forming a whole represented by the national sovereignty that integrated all the American peoples. On the other hand, the Europeans tried to attenuate the American demands, postulating that first there was the salvation of the country that was in danger. Thus, Agustín Argüelles:

... harshly reproached his American colleagues for the attitude of permanently raising particular issues, at a time when European Spaniards, to whom the war left no other possibility than to resist, needed the moral support of American solidarity (Chiaramonti, 2005, 102).

Spirit of body that was recreated with the notion of continental homeland and later, different from the Spanish one, and that would be the cornerstone in the independence processes of the different States in America. Process that would end by establishing the principle of independent authority under the new political powers and where the Congress had political leadership, which was consolidated with a new order designed in the drafting of the Constitution.

This would be another feature of constitutionality, since the experience manifested in Cadiz would contribute to the drafting of the Constitution and to delineate the functioning of the first Peruvian Congress and the Supreme Government Board (1822), in the image of the Spanish Regency Council, which will vary the Hispanic political and legal culture of the time, as foundation of the initiated constitutional process. As for society, on November 9, 1812, the Cadiz constituents approved the decree of abolition of mitas or commandments or repartimientos (Cortes, 1987, p. 3953).

What did not mean its absolute disappearance before the economic difficulties that crossed first the Hispanic administration and later the American one was reestablished.

The Constitution assimilated the category of Indian, Creole, mestizo and caste to that of Spanish, postulating with it a common element to the different corpus with the requirement that they be born free and in the domains of Spain. With this we created the notion of national but being restricted to be elected or representative of the indigenous people living in the New World. In the peninsular and criollos debates, alternatives such as disqualifying the indigenous people due to their short wit and propensity to leisure or to constitute a town without lights, whose representatives will not illustrate the maxims of government (Gálvez, 2004, 313) were handled. The Cortes did not deepen in solving these points, rejected cultural diversity, preferring to keep the Creole as a legal category which continued in the proclamations of independence, except for Buenos Aires, whose statement was written in Spanish and Quechua.

Regarding the church, the experience of the Extraordinary and General Cortes of Cádiz strengthened its political, legal and religious role. The parishes not only constituted the voting centers but also the illustration where the priest mentioned the candidates so that after the homily the representative was elected. In addition, the parish books showed population control with the information of the inhabitants, from baptism and even death. Characteristic that would continue in the right when being a Catholic liberalism, the norms corresponding to filiation, successions and family had to be associated to the ecclesiastical postulate.

In the American case, the situations encountered oscillating positions between the fidelity to the monarch that demanded the return to the state previous to the Bourbon reforms and the rupture with the consequent independence process, an option that was uncertain in its development and political composition. The constitutional monarch personified the regime and acted accompanied by secretaries of State and its discretion was articulated with the Council of State. From here we find the existence of mechanisms limiting the real exercise. The political responsibility was transferred to the secretaries of state with the figure of the endorsement, according to the branch that corresponds.

Sanction whose initiative was taken by the Cortes demanding the formation of cause wherever it may be. Another control mechanism occurred when the legislature denied its consent to the governmental acts foreseen in the fundamental law. Within the existence of these counterweights in the exercise of power the monarch was granted the power to sanction the rule, which could also be denied or observed for which he had thirty days, it being understood that by not sanctioning or pronouncing his amendment was understood as promulgated. Before the parliamentary control, mainly of political control by infraction to the Constitution, the king was prevented from limiting the operation of the collegiate, to suspend it or to dissolve it.

Finally, the Charter provided for the operation of ordinary and extraordinary legislatures, in addition to the establishment of an entity that would act between period and period known as the Permanent Diputacion de Cortes composed of three members of peninsular representatives, three from overseas and one seventh randomly from among the members of the legislature. There is no doubt that the Constitution of 1812 laid the foundations of American constitutionalism and was opening space as a limiting power, not only as rules but in the thinking of philosophers and jurists. They contributed to innovate the rules for the Indian society based not only on the thesis of liberalism but with the fusion of the Indian and Catholic tradition, constituting in this way the preliminary stage to our constitutional history.

After being promulgated, it remained in force with the return of Fernando VII to the throne, who did not accept that his absolutist regime was converted into a constitutional one. The support of 69 deputies allowed him to issue the decree of May 4, 1814, reinstating the Old Regime and nullifying the Constitution. In Peru, again the appointed positions, the inquisition, the mita among others resumed their position. The coup d'état of January 1, 1820 against Fernando VII marked a new stage in the empire. The insurrection led by Lieutenant Colonel Rafael del Riego, in charge of leaving America to defeat the insurgents, made it possible to recast the management of royal power by forcing the monarch to swear the Constitution and therefore submit to his designs during the so-called Liberal Triennium (1820-1823) that allowed the Liberals to be a government and take up immediate measures such as the abolition of the Court of the Holy Office and encourage the development of freedom.

The conservatives opted for a vigilant attitude, complementary to the conspiracies of the monarch, one of which succeeded with the presence of one hundred thousand French troops or the Sons of St. Louis that allowed the restoration of absolutism and therefore the abolition of the Charter in his second life.

IV. THE PROTECTORATE AS A FORM OF GOVERNMENT.

On July 28, 1821, it represents the beginning of the Peruvian State, but also the culmination of the pre-emancipation process that took over after Cádiz the struggle for the political demands of different sectors of the population before the authorities.

Gone were the movements that articulated regions in southern Peru such as the Rebellion of Tupac Catari in Upper Peru and that of the Angulo brothers with Mateo Pumacahua in Cusco and Arequipa, the conspiracies of Indians, mestizos and criollos. The fierce repression of the then viceroys José Fernando de Abascal y Souza (1806-1816) and that of Joaquín de la Pezuela Griñán (1816-1821) allowed the crown to be stabilized until the intervention of José de San Martín and Matorras leading the Argentine expedition and later also Chilean, since 1818.

Until then, the revolts had not managed to break the management of the central power embodied in the viceroy and could be defeated with the support of the royal army, the militias and even the curacas. Situation that presents us that the perception of the emancipation was not uniform, but that it was given mainly of the cities and of the economic zones, especially in the axes of commerce. Process that was articulating to different sectors integrated the protest of the American nations against the Spanish regime, demanding the modification and elimination, in the best of the cases, of their royal measures, but that by not proceeding or doing it delayed they promoted the independence. In the Indian model, Peru and Mexico had represented the bastions of the defense of Hispanicism in America and their fidelity, putting at risk the emancipation of the other political demarcations such as Argentina (Tucumán, July 9, 1816), Chile (Talca, 12 of February of 1818), and the Great Colombia (Angostura, 1819). The liberating expedition of General José de San Martín joined the integrated movements of Spaniards, Creoles, mestizos, Indians, castes and blacks who opted for the decision to guide their own destiny. Since the disembarkation in Pisco, on September 8, 1820, the San Martinian army had the mission to summon the support of the people to legitimize their independence and achieve the adhesion of its inhabitants.

The proclamation of independence in the former intendency of Trujillo on December 29, 1820 was trscendental because it was a remarkable political demarcation after the viceroyalty. To this military actions were added corroborated the strategy of the Liberator, creating the propitious moment to issue the first legal provision of the Peruvian administration: The Provisional Regulation that establishes the demarcation of the territory occupied by the

Argentine-Chilean army, with which they were designed the first departments as well as their first authorities: Department Presidents (later called prefects), the governors, the lieutenant governors, the fiscal agents (controllers), the superior treasury board and the first republican court: The Chamber of Appeals, with headquarters in Trujillo. The confessional character of the political organization that adopted the Catholic religion as a State official was maintained.

The process of changes in Peru demanded the existence of a leader in which the wills of the emancipating people concur, as well as the military and political command (executive and legislative). Reason for which issued the decree of August 4, 1821 that instituted the Protectorate, which covered the gap caused by the founding act of the Peruvian State, designating José de San Martín as head in power. With the Protector of Peru, appears the cabinet of the government integrated by the ministers of State: In the office of State and External Relations Juan García del Río (born in Cartagena de Indias); Guerra and Marina Bernardo Monteagudo (from Tucumán) and Finance, by José Hipólito Unanue y Pavón (born in Arica). The judiciary fell to the High Chamber of Justice, a newly constituted national court. Actions that corresponded to the tenor of the speeches of the Peruvian Liberals that did not cease to postulate the freedom, equality and fraternity of the Declaration of Rights of Man and of the Citizen in this process. Thought that received the words of the new Chief Executive:

"The State of Peru began to exist from the day that the bases of our pact of association were provisionally established" (CDIP 1974, Volume XIII, vol.1, p.249).

This mandate gave beginning to the first militarism that will conclude in 1872 with the ascent of Manuel Pardo, first elected civil president in the office of the

Presidency of the Republic. Meanwhile, the new independent regime declared abolished in all its articles the Constitution of 1812, which was produced politically. Nevertheless, its doctrinal influence continued, being one of the obligatory references of the legislators in the writing of the next constitutional texts and later in the university classrooms.

V. THE FIRST PROVISIONS OF THE BORN PERUVIAN STATE

The new regime was transitory and conditioned to the conjuncture of the war as to the next convocation for the national political representation. Meanwhile, through the Executive, state bases of state design were being established through its decrees, which will be a constant in Peruvian constitutional history, since then, leaving the Judiciary total autonomy, as San Martín himself maintained:

But I will refrain from ever mixing in the solemn exercise of judicial functions, because their independence is the only and true safeguard of the freedom of the people (García Belaunde, 2016, p.9).

After the independence the territorial organization and under the French departmental model that replaced the intendencias and of free parties, existing to February 12, 1821, was added the circumscription of Lima, which included the parties of Yauyos, Cañete, Ica up Nazca. However, this process was altered on April 26, 1822 when the Supreme Delegate José Bernardo Tagle reorganized the physical space with more free parties to give rise to eleven departments, constituting the electoral base that would allow having a national representation, according to the Provisional Regulation that establishes the method for elections ... (Tarazona 1946, pp. 31-38).

The validity of the hostilities of the royalist army in the sierra influenced the composition of the internal demarcations in the paper, responding more to mediatic criteria than to technical ones, probably for granting more legitimacy to the elected ones. The incipient process of emancipation motivated the gradual application of the principles of freedom and equality that had been raised. The governmental discourses, in this sense, demonstrated a proactive will reflected in the decrees in favor of the Indians and the slaves.

6 LA EMANCIPACIÓN EN SUS TEXTOS

ESTADO que manifiesta las siete Intendencias en que está dividido el Virreynato de Lima, con expresión de las Ciudades y Pueblos que comprehenden, número de sus Doctrinas y el de sus habitantes, con distinción de las respectivas clases a que estos corresponden

INTENDENCIAS	PARTIDOS	Ciudades	Villas	Pueblos	Doctrinas	Curatos
Intendencia de Lima	Cercado	1	-	6	14	[illegible]
	Cañete	1	1	[illegible]	7	15
	Ica	1	2	5	[illegible]	12
	Yauyos	-	-	35	7	[illegible]
	Huarochirí	-	-	[illegible]	[illegible]	[illegible]
	Canta	-	-	[illegible]	[illegible]	[illegible]
	Chancay	-	2	[illegible]	9	18
	Santa	-	1	15	7	10
	Total	3	6	[illegible]	[illegible]	[illegible]
Id. de Trujillo	Cercado	1	-	6	[illegible]	[illegible]
	Lambayeque	-	-	7	[illegible]	[illegible]
	Piura	-	-	14	[illegible]	[illegible]
	Cajamarca	-	[illegible]	[illegible]	[illegible]	[illegible]
	Huamachuco	1	-	[illegible]	8	[illegible]
	Pataz	-	-	13	3	[illegible]
	Chachapoyas	-	-	60	[illegible]	[illegible]
	Total	[illegible]	[illegible]	[illegible]	[illegible]	[illegible]

Population by region (Intendance)
PUENTE CANDAMO, José A. (1959) Emancipation in its Texts: The State of Peru. Volume I, p. 6. Lima. Riva-Agüero Institute.

Regarding mita, the independent regime by decree of August 28, 1821, stated: "The service of the Peruvians, known before with the name of Indians or natives did under the denomination of mitas, pongos is extinguished.

"It is abolished the tax that under the denomination of tribute was satisfied to the Spanish Government ... from now on, they will not be denominated to the Indian natives or natural: they are children and citizens of Peru and with the name of Peruvians they must be known".

Decree that, although it sought to revalue this social group, would end up being counterproductive, because if the Indians were citizens, what name would we give to the other sectors that made up that society, whose parameters preserved the Hispanic practices tending to a more corporate community that equal, maintaining the same degree of acceptance and even dependency as can be corroborated in the literature of the time. In the parish registers the Indian denomination was replaced by the Peruvian one, returning to the original term after 1834.

Regarding slavery, the governmental attitude was inclined to dictate devices that did not abolish the institution itself, but acted as palliatives: First, the freedom of wombs established that those born as of July 28, 1821, children of slaves, would be free Second, the drawing of twenty-five individuals, who would be favored with freedom. Third, the enlistment of slaves in the patriot army who after fulfilling of their service would achieve recognition as free men. The consideration of slavery as a consequence of the property rights of the masters made their elimination difficult, since the only possibility was to expropriate the slaves or goods. Practice that as counterpart required the payment of fair compensation to the owners and that at that time could not be made due to the lack of resources of the political legal society.

The government guaranteed the legal order under the norms and customs of the viceroyalty, but also acting as an agent of change introducing, in an incipient manner, the principle of legality to its acts in this diverse reality. Thus, the birth of national law, by its nature, responded to the institutional character not discarding the Roman-canonical tradition neither in its content nor in the procedural part, maintained in the teachings given in the colleges and as in the University of Lima as in their Spanish counterparts, until the middle of the 19th century. The publications of Hispanic texts and their reissues were received in both hemispheres, adding French and exceptionally English, German and Portuguese literature. To this was added the work of the press, called doctrinaire, which became a vehicle for dissemination to the enlightened sectors through transcriptions or reliable translations of contemporary political texts.

The Provisional Statute of October 8, 1821 was the second great norm of this administration. Issued by the Protector for the regime of the free departments, reflected the governmental proposal imposing the institutions and governance of the State in correspondence to the national life, while the Constitution was not dictated. In the first place, it was established who were Peruvian, according to the birth in the territory (ius soli) or through filiation, because they were descendants of Peruvians, which appealed to the use of conventional criteria that linked to nationals. In addition, it was ratified that the official religion of the State would be Catholic, Apostolic and Roman, indispensable requirement to be considered a subject of law and even perform as a public official.

The direction of the State continued under the figure of the Protector, counting on the ownership of political, administrative and military power. For this purpose, the Chief Executive was accompanied by the Ministers of State in their respective branch, empowered to issue resolutions and communications from his office. Responsibility assigned to a holder, who had the obligation to render accounts of the management, originally shared with the Chief Executive, due to the nature of the position. Another creation of this moment was the Council of State, chaired by the Protector of Peru and composed of twelve members: Ministers of State, the general in chief of the army, the chief of staff, three counts, a marquis, the president of the High Chamber of Justice, the Dean of the Cathedral of Lima and a member who would be appointed later. It was an organ of a deliberative nature, especially in exceptional cases.

We can observe that this conformation had the characteristic of being a mixture between the State and civil society when representing different institutions such as the government, the church, the Peruvian nobility and the military force.

On December 2, 1821, the date of the beginning of the sessions of the Council, it was agreed, under the political regime proposed by San Martín, to appoint Juan García del Río and Diego Paroissien to serve on the commission whose purpose was to search for a prince for the Peru among European houses. Although the vocation of Hispanic America was republican, this did not exclude that at times it was sought without monarchical trials to maintain the transition during the process of rupture. The supporters of this position were identified as conservatives, who started from the terror of misgovernment, disorder and probable anarchy, seeing in the monarchical option the guarantee for continuity. It was these who, to justify themselves, maintained that the Americans were not used to command. It is unknown if the monarchical idea of San Martin had been temporary or definitive.

Being in Europe the mission Juan del Rio - James Paroissien, the Protector left the power, which motivated that it varied its original purpose, replacing it by the promotion and diffusion of the mining exploitation and even arranging what would be the first loan of the new State with England worth one million two hundred thousand pounds sterling for the budget of the republic. The Council of State as an institution was reinforced with the delegation of judicial functions assigned by the Regulation for Courts of 1822, and that later would be derived to the Legislative. This transfer of powers, which, although ephemeral, created the conditions for a distortion in the application of the separation of political functions from those that were not.

We can affirm that the emergency circumstances demanded a centralization of functions around the head of government; but after those were finalized, they were not transferred to the corresponding entity but to the Congress, which saw its role strengthened within the state organization. As representative of the Executive within the country we find the President of the Department (Prefect), direct executor of the governmental orders in his jurisdiction, which were complemented with that of his subordinates: the governor and the lieutenant governor. These first indications reveal the existence of nuances in the centralization of functions in a single position, but also in this specific case, the decentralization proposal of a country that still conserved its organization based on the intendencias or regions. Between the first presidencies of department we emphasize the one of Trujillo (Jose Bernardo Tagle), Lima (Jose de la Riva Agüero), Huaylas (Ignacio de Alcázar) and the Coast (Andrés Reyes).

VI. THE PATRIOTIC SOCIETY OF LIMA: MONARCHY OR REPUBLIC

The previous negotiations to the Peruvian State reveal the interest of general San Martin to establish the constitutional monarchical government, provisionally, until the republic was established, a regime in most of the nascent American states. Defender of the monarchy was the secretary and then Minister Bernardo Monteagudo, who considered that the dissemination of liberal ideas in Peru in this process of change was not enough but to prepare the Peruvians, through education and the acceptance of the laws, the defense of their rights and established institutions, against arbitrariness. This would change the perception of Peruvians, meanwhile as a side, the proclamations would help to become aware of the liberal principles that raised independence.

While the government measures were issued, the regime thought it convenient to convene 40 notables from the intelligentsia, the nobility, the bureaucracy and trade to form the Patriotic Society of Lima to discuss the appropriateness of the regime to be adopted, being established on January 10, 1822. Monteagudo embodied San Martin's plan As Secretary of the Liberator, he proposed radical and extreme measures against the Spaniards living in Peru, an attitude that gave him the reputation of having hispanophobia, which would cost him later his expulsion from country in 1822:

... Today it is feared to concede too much power to the rulers, ... but in my opinion it is much more to fear the very little obedience of the governed (CDIP 1974. Volume XIII, Vol. 1, pp. 243 et seq.).

As we see, it was not enough just the assimilation and the conviction of the liberal ideas for the march of the new society because this would only take place to the extent that the people were enlightened. Otherwise, ignorance allowed the authority to become a tyrant, dominating the people without much difficulty. The flexibility of the political theory of Monteagudo illustrates that its variation corresponded to the events of the time. Until then, the adherents to the monarchy seconded by José Ignacio Moreno, José Cavero y Salazar and Hipólito Unanue constituted the majority.

In the opinion of Monteagudo, the Peruvians would progressively become aware - through proclamations - of the principles that independence contributed. Since in Peru was where the spirit of the metropolis was more settled by the number of peninsular residents was incompatible the exercise of democratic ideas in the other groups, socially and racially differentiated. Hence the need to banish all obstacles with the expulsion of the Spanish, and the consequent confiscation of their property. So his first purpose is summarized:

[to] ... erase even the vestiges of that habitual veneration, which men involuntarily pay to those who for a long time have been in possession of making them miserable (Monteagudo, 1823, p.10).

I hate that it reached even those who had sworn Peruvian independence and requested their naturalization letter. Then, Monteagudo argued that not only it was enough to liberate the peoples, but to distinguish the distribution of wealth and the level of preparation of the inhabitants, which complemented freedom. Peru represented a heterogeneous society with determining socioeconomic conditions:

A people that has just been subject to the calamity of following such pernicious habits is incapable of being governed by democratic principles. Nothing matters to change language, as long as the feelings do not change ... (Monteagudo, 1823, p.13).

The third principle inclined to the promotion of public instruction, which would ensure that each inhabitant and citizen knew their duties and rights, becoming the control of the authority. Hence, the need of the regime to found the National Library of Peru and innovate instruction through the Lancasterian teaching method under the direction of Presbyterian James Thompson, who came from Chile and remained in Lima until 1824.

The fourth principle held that the form of government should safeguard the freedom of the individual through the Constitution, limiting the operation of the use of power through three organs. The crystallization of happiness would only occur with a government that promotes the development of work, industry and talents, reducing the social abyss that existed with the majority sectors and where slavery will gradually be abolished, since it constituted a right of patrimonial.

For his part, the cleric José Ignacio Moreno that the situation in which Peru was located did not have the conditions for the implementation of a system that was inclusive, especially when ignorance predominated in the majority sectors. Hence the need for a leader with a strong attitude to act for the welfare of the population, a similar attitude of the monarch in Enlightened Despotism.

Meanwhile, the republican leadership rested in the hands of the lawyer Manuel Pérez de Tudela, who allowed the life of society was based on the happiness product of the exercise of freedom, security and equality that was summarized in the sentence: Firm and Happy for the Union.

Added to this were the arguments that most penetrated the political debate came from another Republican who was not invited to the Society. Under the pseudonym Solitario (lonely) of Sayán, José Faustino Sánchez Carrión (Huamachuco 1787) stood out as the main opponent of the monarchical system, for whom the term was synonymous with decadence while emancipation meant republic. Author of the Letters sent by Solán de Sayán, he maintained that:

The infinite evils that are known in our country are not incurable but because they do not want to apply the appropriate specific, or because they do not take the job of finding the origin that produces them (CDIP, 1974, Volume I, Vol. 9, p. 15).

Their influence through the epistolary relationship with this cenacle or through publications gradually generated changes of position in the members of society. From his Letters, in allusion to Montesquieu and Aristotle, we can infer that the form of government should be based on the territory, customs and character of its inhabitants. The rights could not be defrauded but enjoyed in all the fullness of their exercise; Respecting the principles of freedom, security and property. Sanchez Carrión's phrase "The nation is nothing more than a large family, divided and subdivided into many," evokes the need to articulate each community in the general interest, where each would be responsible for their own destiny to achieve happiness advocated for the illustration. The unadaptability of the monarchical government to the Peruvian State was based on the character of the Peruvians, who were accustomed to receiving what is given, being prone to become vassals and not citizens; although the monarchy was constitutional.

It was necessary to overcome the privileges of the viceregal society by a meritocracy, where by their talents, merits and education individuals would be preferred. The laws were the brakes for the acts of authority and man in society and not the orders of bureaucrats, which became excesses. Although the monarchy was the form of government that had prevailed in history; the notion of Rousseau's social pact had undermined the regime's absolutist tendency. However, the concern for the exercise of freedom was latent and demanded in this concern of a sector of the population, as noted Manuel Lorenzo Vidaurre wondered if all were equal, who obeyed?

Equality, essential for this state construction, was given by legal presumption for all. Although it was argued that sovereignty was rooted in the people, they were enlightened individuals and owners who at that time represented the electoral base, corresponding them as electors and elected. His reference to the thirteen states of the Union in North America made him think that the effectiveness in the management of power would be produced in a federal republic, which also allowed the exercise of different cults while in Peru the religious identification has been Catholic, impeding the profession of another.

The declaration of independence by sections and stages in the national territory, allowed him to think about the American independence. As it is known, it was the parties of Tumbes, Lambayeque and El Cercado in the former intendancy of

Trujillo, who first declared their emancipation; then in the center the party of Huaylas and in the southeast the one of Huamanga. Circumscriptions that later were articulated to the country in 1825, which did not exclude the survival of the power of power elites, local or regional.

On July 12, 1822, the Patriotic Society of Lima concluded its sessions and its president, Bernardo Monteagudo, explained to the Council of State that it had been decided to leave the next Congress to decide on the most convenient form of government. In this way, the monarchist sanmartiniana option failed for the memory of the system of the previous regime, but, nevertheless, the tendency to a republic with strong government and with parliamentary shades survived as we will see later in the following conjunctures.

CHAPTER TWO

Beginnings of constitutionalism

I. THE FIRST CONSTITUENT EXPRESSION: THE CONGRESS OF 1822.

By decree Protector of December 27, 1821 called for elections for the next Constituent Congress with the intention of defining the form of government and prepare the constitution for the country, synonymous with a society that guaranteed their rights and had the separation of powers. This decree established that the powers that "give the peoples to their deputies, will contract exclusively to these objects and will be null those that exceed them".

The Council of State and the Constitution Committee of the Congress were in charge of examining the draft regulation that contemplated the number of voters. For this, the census of the Guide of Outsiders of the year of 1797 with the addition of a deputy for each 15 thousand souls (inhabitants) was used. The electoral process took place after the interviews of the Libertadores José de San Martín and Simón Bolívar in Guayaquil. Documents of the Protector reveal the need to have the Congress and its control mechanisms of political power.

The disapproval of the monarchy as a form of government, had deepened the wear and tear of the regime, adding to it the setback of the war, the deportation of Monteagudo to Chile and tenacious opposition from Lima sectors sympathizers of Republicanism that spoke of King Joseph, alluding to San Martín. Using the parishes as places of suffrage counting as the antecedent elections for the Cortes of 1812, there was the election process for the first national representation that yielded 117 deputies (79 incumbents and 38 substitutes), of which 28 were lawyers and 26 ecclesiastics Above all, in temporary districts because they are still under the control of Viceroy José La Serna. Similar circumstance if we think about the Cadiz experience of 1810.

On the day of the installation, on September 20, 1822, the Protector took the oath of office to the congressmen and, as soon as they assumed their functions, they declared the Legislative Power constituted, residing in it the popular will and exercising it in its name.

General San Martin handed over the political position putting an end to the Protectorate of August 4, which maintained a degree of institutional independence before the convulsed situation by the presence of the realistic army stationed in the mountains. Despite this, it marked the beginning of the Peruvian State, which, incipient since then, was shaping the republican institutions, whose existence combined with the leadership of its leaders or leaders and the notables. Perception that we show in your farewell message:

The presence of a fortunate soldier (no matter how detached he may be) is frightening to the states that are once again constituted ... Peruvians, I leave you the national representation; If you place an entire trust in it, sing the triumph: if not, anarchy will devour you (Bilbao, 1936, p.17).

At the request of Deputy Mariano Arce, José de San Martín was declared:

"Founder of the Freedom of Peru, maintaining the rank of Captain General of Peru and assigning him a salary, which he would resign". (Constituent Congress, 1822, pp.11-12).

The congressmen of 1822 faced with the exercise of a centralized power around the executive and under the influence of political philosophy opted for the opposite alternative, since their grouping was considered as exclusive synonym of representativeness. The direction of the State's business was sought from the Legislative Power, rehearsing a parliamentary governmental formula calling for compliance with the principle of authority. The most lucid and enlightened exponents of viceregal society along with the republicans were in Congress and put the pillars of the legal-political organization of the time. By considering his institution as the first power of the State they made it absorb executive functions, even hindering the end of the war between independents and realists. The Hispanic tradition was adjusting the application of the theory of powers that still maintained a centralized power, but that after the viceroy had not achieved an authority with the same recognition. Making a simile of the French version, the Peruvian deputies opted for the political control of the State including the Chief Executive, who would be elected by the legislators. Liberals were convinced that parliamentarism was the best option for the State, hence for the direction of state business determined the birth of a collegiate Executive called the Governing Board or the French consulate, whose provisions resemble the Spanish Regency Council, as we have argued above.

This represented a delegated commission of the Congress, composed by the deputies Jose La Mar (ex- governor of Callao), Felipe Antonio Alvarado (ex-mayor of Lima) and Manuel Salazar y Baquíjano, count of Vista Florida, with the purpose of assuming the command of the campaigns against the royalist troops. The decree creating the Junta Gubernativa, of September 21, 1822, also stated that:

"3º This commission will take turns among individuals of the Congress; 4º The elected ones are separated from the Congress, after they lend the respective oath; 5º This commission will consult the Congress in the diplomatic business and any others" (García Belaunde, 2016, p. 113).

The executive function was shared with the Secretaries of State, who replaced the ministers. Again, the strength of the Legislative and the march of the

Peruvian State were conditioned to the future of the war for independence and the adhesion of the inhabitants in the territories still dominated by the viceroy from Cusco. The Congress tried to involve the Indian communities in the exceptional event that implied independence and the struggle against the Spaniards. Through proclamations written in Quechua they were made aware of the benefit of this political project. In this aspect, the way they proceeded was not different from the eighteenth-century Carolino model: Everything for the people, but without the people outlining social and then economic reforms:
"You Indians, you are the first objective of our care, we remember what you have suffered and we work to make you happy in the day: You are going to be noble, educated, owners and you will represent among men all that is due to your virtues" (Rivet and Créqui-Monfort, 1952, Volume I, p. 287).

In that sense, the pretension of the legislators of the United Provinces of Rio de La Plata was more involved in drafting the act of independence in bilingual form. The direction of the march of the Peruvian Legislative was possible through the operation of the Directing or Permanent Tables and their commissions established by thematic order: Bases of the Constitution, Constitution, Fine Arts, Commerce, Travel Allowance and Budget, Diplomatic, Special Treasury and Commerce, Statistics, War, Education and Public Health, Legislation, Freedom of Printing, Justice, Treasury, Memorials, Mining, Police, Powers, Prizes and Agriculture, Regulation and Visit to prisons.
The functionality of the government under the version of the supreme junta soon showed evidence of its inoperability, since being a delegated commission, it lacked faculties beyond those stipulated. The real and effective power was absent and the failure before the First Expedition of Intermediates caused that a sector of the army led by the general Andrés Santa Cruz and Calahumana gave

the first Coup, on February 26, 1822, imposing the aristocrat José Mariano of the Riva Agüero and Sánchez Boquete, Marquis of Montealegre de Aulestia as the first president of Peru:

"Balconcillo, is therefore ... an episode of deep repercussions, not only immediate but future, in the national life, because in Balconcillo the case, repeated in our history, of the military uprisings is given for the first time" (Ravago, 1959, p.52).

This first crisis of governability or coup d'etat we can see the close correlation in the mutiny or the declaration of Aznapuquio when General José La Serna, supported by a section of the army, pressured the viceroy Joaquín de la Pezuela to name him general in chief and resign. This as a consequence of its weakness in the negotiations with San Martin, prior to Peruvian independence. Francisco Javier Luna Pizarro, president of the Congress resigned and moved to Chile. Riva Agüero, former colonel of militias and then of the army had the consent of a sector of Lima society and had served as Prefect of the Department of Lima. Riva-Agüero, who was also a lawyer, was elevated as Supreme Chief of the Armed Forces, opting to grant him the maximum military grade so as not to have difficulty with the institutes he had to lead, a thought that would last until the 20th century and be reproduced with the then commander Luis M. Sánchez Cerro.

The government, with the support of the army, devoted itself to continue the campaign, while the Legislative Power continued with the drafting of the political letter that would be added to the transitory provisions of San Martín.

II. THE CRISIS OF GOVERNMENT: TWO PRESIDENTS OF THE REPUBLIC

The government led by José de la Riva-Agüero had a gravitational failure with the loss of the II Intermediate Campaign, putting at risk the advances of the independent administration. The realistic counteroffensive unleashed its responsibility before the Congress that chose to dismiss him on June 23, 1823. Faced with the fear of the royalist occupation of the capital, the Legislative moved to the castle of Real Felipe. The defenestrado ex-president left for Trujillo with some employees and members of Congress who were loyal to him. Meanwhile, the party that remained in Callao appointed José Bernardo Tagle, Marquis of Torre Tagle as the second president of Peru. Circumstance that showed in the Peruvian territory three administrations: two of them independent and the viceregal government with headquarters in the city of Cusco.

Riva Agüero with related members established in the north the Senate chaired also by him, whose members corresponded to the ten departments established for the elections of 1822. Hipólito Unanue, served as vice president of the House and senator for Tarma. Despite the friendship with the de facto president, the deterioration of the political situation prevailed due to the increase in instability, abandoning this adventure to return to Lima. With the resumed sessions on August 6, the Congress took urgent measures: The sending of a commission formed by deputies Joaquín Olmedo and José Faustino Sánchez Carrión to invite the Liberator Simón Bolívar to conclude the emancipation. Second, approve the Constitution and confirm José Bernardo Tagle as the sole president of the Republic, which took place on August 16, 1823.

Bolivar, who first sent a contingent at the disposal of the Peruvian congress of three thousand Gran Colombians with Antonio José de Sucre at the head, arrived on September 1 of the same year and was able to perceive the political fragility through which the country was passing. As an immediate measure, the Legislature granted him military command and also persecuted the outlawed Riva-Agüero. In as much in the political thing, the Political Constitution of the State was promulgated the 12 of November of 1823, whose use was conditioned to the establishment of the Dictatorship of the following year, soon by the dación of the Constitution of 1826 while it governed and finally until it was replaced in its entirety by the following Letter.

III. THE CONSTITUTION OF 1823

Having as background the Bases of the Constitution, of December 17, 1822 and the doctrine of the Spanish Constitution of 1812, the Constitution Committee finally finished writing and the full approval of the first national text. Inspired by the social contract or pact, the Charter had the purpose of promoting the unity of the different sectors that made up the Peruvian State. It imposed the first constitutional state design that conjugated the political organization, coming from the Hispanic and French influence with our idiosyncrasy. Established compliance with the authority, embodied in his articles the idea of the Peruvian nation as a starting point to gather around him all the inhabitants where the political organization had jurisdiction. Under the Gallic thinking of the nation state, its similar Peruvian was built on the Creole identity, assimilating the religion and Castilian language that would survive until the twentieth century, under a liberal perspective that was also racial.

The exercise of the electoral power was assigned under the supervision of the Congress, the same one that would be developed by complementing the elections held for the election of the Deputies coming from the parochial electoral colleges in the Cadiz way. The system was indirect and concluded with the scrutiny of the minutes by the Legislature, as a guarantee against possible mistakes in case it was a direct version. The President of the Republic was elected by Congress and therefore gave an account of his actions in political and military matters of the Republic before him. Fact that refers us to the parliamentary system, where the government comes from, but with the peculiarity that did not include the ministers.

The congress was constituted in its origin in a unicameral manner. A mechanism for the renewal of the congressmen by half was planned every two years; although this would not prevent the presence of local or regional leaders within the Congress, placing above the technical criterion the individual nature. Only members of Congress enjoyed the right of initiative of the laws, an argument that was based on the belief that a pluripersonal institution would be the guarantee that the norm retained the characteristics of abstraction, impersonality and infallibility.

There was the Conservative Senate, an entity separate from the Legislative, whose members were elected by the provinces, three being by department (two incumbents and one alternate). These were the guardians of the Constitution and appointed public officials (civil and ecclesiastical). He was authorized to make accusations against the Chief Executive, the ministers and members of the Supreme Court of Justice for breach of the Constitution. The requirement to be a senator shows that few voters would qualify because it was necessary to own a property whose value exceeded 10 thousand pesos or an income of 2,000. Finally, the term of office was twelve years and the members could be lay or ecclesiastical, in which case the number was limited to six.

With regard to the Executive and after the experience the Supreme Government Board, the legislators opted for the figure of the President of the Republic, accompanied by the vice president. Once his appointments were made by the Congress of the Republic, the president proceeded to appoint his ministers. Both he and his senior officials had political responsibility for their actions.

As a government, it brought together the national bureaucracy (civil and ecclesiastical) as well as the armed force, being a requirement for admission, in addition to the abilities or capacities of the respective office, to be Catholic. From the San Martinian experience, it was established that the ministers were the highest political officials in the corresponding branch, the oldest of which being Foreign Affairs, a tradition that is preserved in the protocols up to the present.

The Constitution established the need to limit the power of the president and even more that was not hereditary or for life (ahead of criteria that would perpetuate the exercise of power). It was decided to prevent immediate re-election to said position. In the exercise of the public function, the requirement of Peruvian nationality began to be outlined, either by birth in the territory, filial link or by naturalization, a restriction that opposed continental Americanism, still in force in the performance of Peruvian political or military positions: Joaquín Olmedo (Guayaquil), José La Mar (Cuenca), José de Santa Cruz (La Paz) etc. The vice president would assume the functions in substitution of the president, in case of death, resignation or dismissal and in the absence of this, it was up to the President of the Senate to hold the functions until the next election.

The promulgated Constitution that hoisted the independence liberalism imposed the formality under the revolutionary discourse, but at the same time used the Hispanic custom in the content as the implementation of the Bourbon reforms continued under the proposal of the citizen-president. Liberalism that was opening the way to the imposition of the law as a source of the right initiated since the proclamations of San Martín, which would be supplemented by custom, doctrine and jurisprudence. Process that would be produced gradually in the places where the Peruvian State had a presence. In the interim of moving from one regime to another, it was decided to strengthen the Peruvian State link within a mentality that posited political organization only as authority.

Independence demanded the artificial creation of habits, as in France, that would encourage committed behavior with the country, for which the Congress created icons that would bring the population closer to this great epic that implied independence and taking as reference a significant event in the style of the French revolutionaries:

"Institute national holidays to maintain the civic union, stoke patriotism and perpetuate the memory of the most famous events of national independence." (García Belaunde 2017, p. 134)

The Charter of 1823 recognized universal suffrage for all who qualify as citizens, being necessary to be a national (by birth in the territory or by filiation), be over 25 years old-age that came from the Roman-canonical tradition or married, have a property, especially real estate, exercise a profession or trade useful in the industry and finally be independent. In principle, the requirement to know how to read or write was suspended until 1840. For public jobs as for political positions it was essential to be Catholic, in addition to fulfilling the corresponding requirements. As we indicated, the system of elections was indirect based on the parochial and provincial electoral colleges for the election of congressional representatives.

The judicial body was designed taking as the highest instance in the administration of justice to the Supreme Court of the Republic and reference to the former Real Audiencia de Lima of 1542. housing judges and prosecutors in the same institution. The Court of Appeals of Trujillo and the High Chamber of Justice, respectively, had remained behind. Located in the capital of the republic, its headquarters was itinerant between the Government Palace and one of the environments of the Court of the Holy Office or the Holy Inquisition. It was composed of a president, eight members and two prosecutors, acting at the national level as a court of last resort.

Subsequently, the upper courts continued in the nascent departments or former municipalities: Arequipa, Cusco, Huamanga, Huancavelica, Puno, Tarma, Trujillo and Lima. Of these only the last two were under independent authority. They were composed of attorneys and prosecutors. Then there were the judges of first instance or of law and finally the justices of peace, in the civil as in the military. In this last one, Solicitor General was even instituted within the military commission for prisoners.

As I have indicated in a previous work (Gálvez, 2017), the military causes in the first instance were in charge of a general in chief and the war auditor, who was a civilian. Acting ultimately the High Chamber of Justice, through two of its members, assisted by a general (Law of December 23, 1822).

IV. BOLÍVAR, FATHER AND THE FIRST SAVIOR OF PERU

Meanwhile, the structural crisis of Peru continued and only a set of strategies in the military and political context would put an end to the instability. Riva-Agüero was ordered to be arrested by his lieutenant Colonel Antonio Gutiérrez de la Fuente, who, instead of executing the order, deported him. The insurrection of Argentine military in the Real Felipe for being unpaid deepened the situation of the capital, and the Congress delivered the dictatorial power to the Liberator President of Colombia Simón Bolívar by Law of February 10, 1824:

"4 ° The Liberator may suspend the constitutional articles, laws and decrees that are in opposition to the requirement of the public good in the present circumstances and in those that may arise, as well as decreeing in use of the authority exercised, everything concerning the organization of the Republic. "With the triumphs in the battles of Junín (August 6) and then Ayacucho (December 9) that consolidated the independence and put an end to the military rule in Peru, the circumstances that led to the recess of Congress were declared closed and the dictator decreed his reinstatement on February 10, 1825. However, the legislators believing that their inspection work could hinder the actions undertaken by the Liberator, decided to submit to his plans, especially when his personality was overwhelming, which is why he was granted the title of Father and Savior of Peru".

Title that reminds us of the king Despot Illustrated, father of all, who wanted welfare for the people, but without his consent but unlike him, the congress, composed of the elite and enlightened that knew of political theory, gave him the faculties without greater control by the media perception, forgetting that Bolívar with more talents than others, was no stranger to concentrating power. A transfer of power that goes back to Rome and then recreated by liberalism within representative democracy. A way of thinking that has survived not only in contemporary dictatorships, but that we show in general elections, especially when the representative system currently inclusive admits illiterate representatives, who make the most transcendental decisions in the country.

Outside of Lima, the separation of Upper Peru and the birth of Bolivia as a State added to the capitulation of General Ramon Rodil in Callao, the last authority in the service of the Spanish monarchy, constituted the events that added to the management of Bolivar. During the legislature of 1826, 52 of the deputies elected for the legislature of that year signed a document requesting the Liberator to suspend the convocation for a period of one year, convinced that a strong arm would impose the principle of equality before the law. Circumstance that created estrangement from a sector of the electorate and the Governing Council led by General Andrés Santa Cruz authorized the Supreme Court to examine and rate the candidates for Deputies:

In Simon Bolivar's mentality were the interest in achieving political recognition of the United States of America, England and France from the nations emancipated by him. This was followed by the Amphictyonic Congress of Panama, the Spanish-American integration block project and the Federation of the Andes, where the Liberator, as Head of State would not have political responsibility:

"The President of the Republic comes to be in our Constitution as the Sun that signs in its center, gives life to the Universe. This supreme authority must be perpetual because in systems without hierarchies they need more than in others, a point around which citizens turn their magistrates "(Pareja, 1951, p 41).

The support of the Bolivarian proposals demanded the existence of a tradition and habits that were absent in the government. It was necessary to create political institutions that would prevent tyranny and ignorance. No one can deny that, in its own way, it was an alternative that reconciled the exercise of freedom with stability and right with internal peace, but that counted on opponents such as Ramón Castilla or Mariano Alejo Álvarez.

The transition from one political regime to another through a revolution did not end with the establishment of democracy, since it did not mean an obligatory sequence, which showed the contradiction of the promise made by Bolívar on March 11, 1824 in the sense that after the triumph would return to Colombia leaving Peru free. There was no natural democratization that has given an immediate redistribution of wealth, which can lead us to affirm the need for a stage before this as was liberalism.

Unlike San Martinian management, the Bolivarian wanted to set a precedent with a liberal individualist design, generating a contradiction with the freedoms it sought to protect by issuing norms that collided with Andean traditions, of a communal nature. It was as well as the property like the indigenous organization that had been assimilated in the Indian Right during the viceroyalty, they were put under the legalistic analysis -especially French- that went against everything considered corporate, being understood as synonymous of privilege. Parameters that did not conform to the ayllu, linked by kinship ties, by the use of labor through mita or ayni, or by the vertical nature of the land. Fact that shows us the distancing of the State in this cultural issue. Simón Bolívar ordered, by decree of April 8, 1824, the distribution of community lands:

"Article 2 ° Declare land owners to the so-called Indians, with free disposition of them. Article 3 ... the so-called community lands will be distributed according to the ordinance among all Indians who do not enjoy any other land, being the owner of it ... and selling the surplus ... Article 4 This will be done repartimiento with consideration to the state (civil) of each personero ... "(Congress of the Republic, 2000a)

Later, the law of July 4, 1825, provided that the caciques (or curacas) were usurpers of the lands of the Indians and therefore were not recognized the authority, likewise the lands had to be distributed among the members of this group. This measure created a serious problem in rural areas by removing protection from the parcels of the comuneros. The recognition of the figure of the community was not framed with the governmental legal figures. To this we only add that this was the application of the thesis of John Locke, who considered the individual as owner, which in the recent United States of North America meant a farmer an owner, but in a country like the Andean said speech would not enjoy of the same implications since ancestrally the property had been communal and linked to a mode of organization, that although its foundation was the land, this did not exclude a level of authority as well as the presence of cultural elements that converged around it. With Hipólito Unanue as president of the Council of Government, the payment of a direct tribute that the Indians would pay to the State was resumed by decree of August 11, 1826:
"The corresponding contribution to the natives will be reduced to the same amounts, terms and circumstances in which the year 1820 was established." (Congress of the Republic, 2000a).

It is interesting to note that this proposal came from the prefecture of Cuzco, which, although it does not have the heading, was General Agustín Gamarra, who repeated the discourse of idleness of the oidor Juan de Matienzo of 1567, to force the Indian to work. forced, in the medieval style of Castile.
These measures portray the imposition of a system to get closer to the Western model without considering human capital as the material. A governmental process of ignorance of indigenous communities and the postponement of cultural diversity under the Creole scheme, in force until the twentieth century

and that would have a significant break point with the reincorporation of indigenous communities as their lands in the Charter of 1920 during the regime of Augusto Bernardino Leguía. The Liberator wanted to individualize the property without considering the rotation of crops or the use of resources in communal form or in several verticalities (notion of ecological floors)

On June 1, 1826, it was established that government management was assisted by the new version of the Governing Council formed by the ministers: José María de Pando, in the portfolio of Foreign Affairs and Interior; Hipólito Unanue first head of the office of Justice and Ecclesiastical Business, José de Larrea and Loredo in the Treasury and interim José Mercedes Castañeda, in the portfolio of War and Navy; one of which served as president. The council had deliberative character in difficult cases, being able to assume the business of the government when the dictator marched to provinces. Support was given to the figure of the secretary general, spokesman for the chief executive, whose existence would be repeated later in another de facto government.

III. THE LETTRE OF 1826 OR LIFE CONSTITUTION

Known also as the Bolivarian Charter, had among its inputs the French Constitution of the year VIII, as well as the doctrine and the epistolary relationship of the Liberator with the French liberal Benjamin Constant. It proposed as an articulating axis the creation of an electoral power where citizens elected a voter for every hundred. In its original version, the electors of their constituency chose their representatives for the commune, a practice that was carried out later in the department, where from a list of ten people, the most suitable ones were chosen in the performance of the public function in the provincial, departmental and national level. The electors formed the so-called electoral bodies with a duration of 4 years and qualified the citizens for the different political positions. Unlike the Constitution of Napoleon, that of Bolivar was based on the figure of the departments, the base of the electoral college was the party, the subdelegation or the corregimiento of Indians.

Along with this power we find the Legislative (integrated by three chambers: tribunes, senators and censors), the Executive (with a president for life, a vice president and four secretaries of State) and the Judicial (with the same organization of the Constitution of 1823). Thus, the elections became the guarantee to legitimize the existence of a strong government and an expanded congress that moved away from the oligarchic profile molded from the previous letter. Twenty-four members formed each of the three legislative chambers. The Congress enjoyed general powers as a whole to define the appointment of the President of the Republic for the first time, confirm his successor, approve the appointment of the vice president and designate the candidates proposed by the polling stations.

He was in charge of starting the process for political responsibility against the Vice President of the Republic, the Secretaries of State and the members of the chambers themselves. The Tribunes were renewed every four years and their members had to be at least twenty-five years old. Finally, the Censors that constituted the conservative chamber of the Legislative. Its members as well as being able citizens must have at least forty years of age and have no criminal record. They were attributed the political and moral power of the system. If it was deemed convenient, it was this chamber that was in charge of the impeachment and the case would be considered by the three chambers.

The President of the Republic was the Chief Executive and his position was of a life-time nature. He must be a native of Peru with more than thirty years, have no criminal record, have provided important services to the nation and have known talents in the administration of the State, requirements that limited a majority application. By special law it was stipulated that the liberators were Peruvian, modifying in this way the requirement of nationality and then that of citizenship so as not to be incompatible with the performance of the position (Decree signed by José María de Pando, Minister of the Interior, Council of the Republic Peruvian, Lima, November 30, 1826).

The president proposed the vice president of the Republic, who would be his successor and the four secretaries of state. He lacked the power to appoint political authorities, hence he could not be considered absolutist. The president for life was not responsible for any act of his administration so the legislature could not take account, which did not happen with the vice president who was subject to control for enjoying direct political exercise with the Secretaries of State. These high-ranking officials, although they could act with full independence, did so according to the will of the president. Considered a regime of egalitarian Caesarism, the life version of power was soon questioned by the American reality presenting it as legalized caudillismo or peculiar form of republic, which responded to the lack of tradition or habit of government, lacking in capable figures or prestige.

Under the Creole parameter, the strengthening of the Peruvian Nation was strengthened, as a meeting of all the individuals, which was not the heritage of anyone with the purpose of declaring a political cohesion among the inhabitants. In spite of this, regionalisms were still preserved, where the notables (mining entrepreneurs, landowners, priests, among others) dominated. In the territorial scope, the Charter of 1826, similar to the Provisional Regulations of 1821, was the first to expressly indicate the departmental demarcation conformed by: La Libertad, Arequipa, Lima, Junín, Cuzco, Ayacucho and Puno. Extensions that in the XXI century could be macroregions.

Regarding the identification of the State with the Catholic religion, although it was retained, the impediment of another was not expressly indicated but it would lack state protection. On the other hand, the appointments for the different members of the clergy were made through short lists. The electoral college proposed priests, vicars and bishops. On June 1, 1826 the Executive went to the polling stations to approve the Life Constitution and appoint Bolivar, its president. Circumstance that is presented to us as a popular consultation, the same that was not provided for by law, since the doctrinal interference was inclined towards congressional consent due to its deliberative nature. For Pando (1998), this was the only way out before the dissolution of the Congress of the 26th, in his opinion it was not so true that the schools did not possess such power in rigor of principles:

"Even if the electoral colleges want to be accused of being composed of degraded beings who blindly followed the impulse given to them, it can not be conceived how in all of Peru not a generous voice was raised up that would vituperate their conduct" (p. 250).

The Charter was approved by 58 polling stations of the polling stations in a similar way than in Bolivia and the Council of State being sworn in on the 9th of the following month. There was a minority La Gran Colombia, through its military, presented itself as a hegemonic state that far from having empathy, did not articulate with its similar and respective authorities. Although heterogeneity was the basis for the federation, the ignorance of the potential of the leader leaders of a nationalist tendency and the way in which this integration was applied ended up subtracting legitimacy from the project of the Federation of the Andes.

IV. THE CONSTITUTION OF 1828, THE MOTHER OF ALL THE CONSTITUTIONS

Under this name, José Pareja Paz Soldán (1951) baptized the letter that dealt with a first moment of constitutional maturity, since it better adapted the political theory of the time to a projection of Peruvian reality. Let's see his background. The end of the Bolivarian regime was also that of its Constitution and also that of those close to the Liberator, temporarily because the political class was very small. The absence of Bolivar gave rise to a meeting of notables, on behalf of the neighbors, to denounce that the polling stations lacked powers for the approval of the fundamental law and therefore sued before the Council of Government, in charge of Andrés de Santa Cruz, the convocation of elections for the Constituent Congress to pronounce on said text, adding also the designation of the chief executive. Circumstances forced the holder to declare the lifetime constitution abolished and to restore the 1823 constitution.

Pando, defender of the previous regime, disengaged his participation, arguing that the new polling stations would have an expedited right for the appointment of the new representatives since they possessed the true national will and on the other hand he pointed out that Bolívar: ... could not have been in charge of a constitutional magistracy incompatible with his status as a Colombian citizen

and president of that Republic (Pando, 1995, 253). However, Pando himself had signed a decree, days before promulgating the new constitution, which granted the liberators Peruvian nationality. It required a greater refinement of state institutions, meanwhile the conjuncture again allowed the appearance of the capital city council, since 1822 and that met the will of a neighborhood sector.
The experience produced in the previous regime required amending the juridical-political rules and to that purpose, the Congress was constitutional and not ordinary, since the new measures required that the voters leave aside the daily regulation of the country. Installed on June 4, 1827, the Legislative Branch had 87 Deputies and 25 substitutes elected by province, including the territory of Maynas that had joined the department of La Libertad. Again, Javier Luna Pizarro was the president of the Congress and before him Andrés Santa Cruz handed over the power. Days later, the law was passed through which the President of the Republic and his vice-president would assume the positions as holders.

In that same permanent session Luna Pizarro proposed José La Mar and Cortazar and Manuel Salazar and Baquíjano, former members of the Governing Board, to fill these positions. We must understand that the haste in the appointments was due to the desire to stop the leadership of Santa Cruz, whose sympathizers disclosed their position in a letter of the time. Pareja Paz Soldán poses in reflection the legitimacy of the act:
"Can there be president and vice-president owners without having formed the Constitution that is the legal origin of these leaders? Can he get out of its bosom those who occupy these high ranks without bringing the note to try an oligarchy? "(Pareja, 1951, 49).

CONSTITUCION POLITICA

REPUBLICA PERUANA.

CONGRESO JENERAL CONSTITUYENTE,

1828

LIMA,

The Constitution of 1828, the mother of all Peruvians Constitutions.

On the one hand, the Constitution of 1823 was in force again and the Congress was constituent and therefore could proceed in this way, placing itself above the law stipulating that appointments should be made by the polling stations. It was decided to do it from the Legislative Power, even more if the aforementioned norm had not been promulgated. The impact of the designation of La Mar was not to the liking of military sectors and other regions of the country, because it was questioned the nationality of the new president who never hid his origin, because he was born in Cuenca (territory under sovereignty of the Gran Colombia and before Audiencia de Quito).

He enjoyed the condition of Peruvian for the services rendered to the independence and that concluded with the battle of Ayacucho according to the law of February 12, 1825. Condition that Bolivar himself had by later norm. However, the emersion of nationalism in the military sectors like that of General Agustín Gamarra in the provinces of Quispicanchis and Urubamba of Cuzco soon became a disobedience to authority. On the other hand, the Peruvian State officially communicated to the Liberator the installation of said Legislative, the nullity of the Charter of 1826 as well as the election of the highest authorities of the Executive as owners.

In response to the caesarismo or ascent of Simón Bolívar, the legislators opted for the North American regime as at the time it was the French liberal Alexis de Tocqueville in his work Democracy in America, hence they preferred American presidentialism and the federal system. The republic continued as a form of government under a strong political leadership embodied in the Chief Executive, without the need for the office to be for life, bringing together the Head of State, Government, the General Administration of the Republic, as well as the armed forces. Moreover, the office allowed immediate reelection for a further period, which at that time was four years.

"The figure of the vice president was maintained, who only possessed the corresponding powers to replace the incumbent due to physical or moral impossibility or when he leaves for the campaign" (García Belaunde, 2016, 166).

The governmental efforts were accompanied by the Ministers of State, who signed the decrees and orders of the president in his office, producing the shared political responsibility since the holder assumed it as the high officials with the ministerial endorsement. he Charter of 1828 indicated the initiative in the elaboration of laws in charge of the ministers, leaving also open the possibility of creating more ministerial offices as indicated by law.

The bicamerality was incorporated into the Legislative, consisting of two chambers; that of deputies, representatives of the provinces, whose members varied according to the proportion of the electors, and that of senators at the rate of three per department. The age (26 for the first and 40 for the second), have property or possession of a capital that produces a certain annual income; like being a neighbor and resident of the parish.

The Constitution of 1828, in addition to the American influence, had the French one based on the principle of legality and on the limitation of rights, with the object of legal culture being more legalistic, not being able to generate a right by judicial interpretation. As a political organization, more value was given to nationality by territory (ius soli) than to filiation as a son of a Peruvian father and / or mother (ius sanguini) and to nationality for foreigners. To these requirements that will form the census vote or with requirements, it was added that the individual must be over 21 years of age, demonstrate residence for a decade in the country; to be married, widowed or ecclesiastical and to own a property of twelve thousand pesos or a capital that produced thousand.

From the previous letters, the accusatory power for the violation of the Constitution rested in the Chamber of Deputies only in this version was before the Senate and involved the members of the Executive, both legislative chambers and the supreme members. The second chamber resolved whether or not there was cause for accusations. Before the parliamentary recess, the Charter foresaw the establishment of the Council of State, former Conservative Senate of

1823. It was composed of ten senators who replaced the ministers of the State and trusted personnel of the Executive. Led by the vice president of the Republic or failing that by the president of the Senate. It was responsible for ensuring compliance with the Constitution and the laws; He had fiscal and administrative deliberative powers. Institution that limited the excess of power of the current ruler, who in his probable anxiety would pretend to exercise control in the other areas of the State as happened with the Bolivarian experience.

This also prevented the formation of imposed supranational units, which motivated the liberals to return to the idea of the exercise of power in shared spaces adding to it the control between organs with the concurrence of the departments. A sector of the legislators was betting on a federal demarcation, similar to the North American model. Historically, in Peru it had always been conceived from an axis: Cusco (Incas), Lima (viceroyalty) from which the geo-space was consolidated and dominated the territory with the other demarcations. The conservatives were inclined towards the unitary alternative that favored a strong government, under the thought that in this way it would avoid falling into the hegemony of powers of the local elites. Thus, the belief that a federated republic inspired by a sovereignty closer to the people succumbed to the centralized model in Lima, but with the collaboration of departments that had more resources than the capital itself.

In their defense, the liberals concluded that centralism could give rise to new forms of despotism; but also, it was conscious that the moment was not opportune to be federal for lack of resources and money, as it maintained Manuel Lorenzo Vidaurre (1827):

"If today the state is divided, the government does not have that amount that is indispensable to attend to security and the public good. We are neither safe nor happy. None of our departments is so strong that it can sustain a sudden attack on its own and without the help of others "(p. 8).

The new Constitution settled the unitary republican regime; However, it was not an obstacle for other ways to pretend in the future and the style of the time, to propose integration under Confederation (1836), the federal version of Nicolás de Piérola (1899) and even in the Constituent Assembly (1978-79). The legislators considered that the balance of power with the Executive was not only a matter for the Congress but could be done through the Departmental Boards, from which the next candidates of the state authorities would come.

Under the decentralist thought the municipality also returned, as an institution that strengthened the link between the people and sovereignty, manifested with actions in favor of the locality. The boards promoted the interests of the department in general: among which were examining the accounts of the municipal bodies, presenting candidates in double lists for prefect, subprefects and governors to the Executive and bring civilization to the bordering wild tribes of the department. Approach that offers us to show that the imposition of one culture on the others continued under the Catholic Creole profile.

The presidential mandate of General Agustín Gamarra (1829-1833) demonstrated how the leadership of the caudillo overcame the power of the Departmental Juntas, subjecting them to the appointment of soldiers in the different prefectures. Thus, the decentralization advocated by the conservatives ended up establishing a short centralism between the national government and the departmental one, questioning the apparent triumph of Peruvian liberalism in the state organization. Quickly change the conduct of society and the previous political regime under criticism against despotism and the arbitrariness that he represented. Undoubtedly, more mechanisms were needed to balance the management of power in this incipient State.

An important change was the granting of citizenship to every free man over 21 years of age or married, born in Peruvian territory, even if they were illiterate and foreigners who served the patriotic ranks or who had lived in Peru since 1820. With this, the legislators moved away from the census vote. In this way, the requirements for the exercise of being a lawyer, profession or industry, rent and property were withdrawn, especially until the respective registration of the latter was drawn up. The influence of a confessional State maintained the protagonism of the parish as an administrative unit for the management of the demographic information of that time (baptism, religious marriage and deaths) but also as a voting center for the election of the polling stations. They formed the first instance to then form the provincial colleges that elected the President of the Republic by an absolute majority.

The minutes of the suffrage were to be opened and qualified by Congress. It was this body that finally proclaimed the winning candidate by an absolute majority; the others with the greatest number of votes remained for the election of the vice president. By way of control, the Charter of 1828 provided for the Congress to appoint a special tribunal composed of 7 judges (known in slang as the court of 7 bones) to oversee the Supreme Court members, who were appointed by Congress. Regarding rights, the Charter introduced new ones: The inviolability of the secrecy of correspondence and property rights, the right to a good reputation, the freedom to work, the right to petition, and the right to primary education, consolidating the tendency of the express powers.

The ideologists of 1828 created a Constitution that would govern for five years at the end of which a National Convention should be convened to write the final letter because there was hope to capture the general regime. Meanwhile, the State through the Congress proceeded with the task of establishing the border limits, this time with Bolivia, which was recognized as independent. The national Executive was charged with entering into negotiations with that country provided that it was carried out with its own government. The Constituent Congress entered into recess on June 17, 1828, meanwhile the permanent commission was established, made up of three deputies by department.

The Permanent Commission received five attributions in this interim: Dispatch the files processed before the Congress, supervise the fulfillment of the Constitution and the law, qualify the minutes of the elections of the deputies, elect the senators and present bills to the Congress.

The report of this commission would later reveal the details that occurred to fulfill its mission: The extension of powers given by the government to the prefects in the electoral process, the lack of voter registration lists for their disclosure, the declaration of total nullity of the elections produced in Trujillo, the denunciation of alleged infractions of the law by the supreme members, the nullity of the elections for deputies in Urubamba, Chucuito, Paucartambo, Moquegua, Conchucos-Bajo, Tayacaja, Huancané, Calca, Tambobamba, Condesuyos , Castrovirreyna, Huanta, Huamanga, Cangallo, Huanuco and Pasco, the partial nullity in Jauja of one of the proprietary representatives and of all the substitutes. We can argue that the contribution of the legislators strengthened this incipient constitutionalism giving rise to the famous phrase pronounced by José Pareja Paz Soldán (1951):

"... the Letter of 1828 deserves the title of mother of our Constitutions, since all subsequent ones, that of 1834, 1839, 1856, 1860, 1867 and 1920 are, in ... judgment [of Manuel Vicente Villarán], legitimate daughters more or less similar to the common mother ... "(p.59).

On the other hand, the partial reception of the minutes for senators was subject to the date of elections, taking place first in the departments of Lima, Arequipa and La Libertad on February 10, 1829, which would occur later in Ayacucho, Cusco and Puno. Finally, months later, on August 31, Congress was installed with their respective cameras. Before the coup d'état that deprived Marshal La Mar of the presidential power, the circumstances demanded that the government could not remain headless, which the congress corrected with the appointment of Agustín Gamarra and Luis Antonio Gutiérrez de la Fuente as president and vice-president of the Republic, acting as interim. Later, the election confirmed the role of Gamarra, who held the first magistracy while La Fuente, despite not having an absolute majority, ended up defeating José María de Pando in the elections.

This began a new mandate on December 20, 1829 for four years, testing the institutionality of the country. During this period there were up to 17 attempts at rebellion against the regime, demonstrating the degree of conflict with the Executive. Meanwhile the Legislative continued in its debates with the control of the political institutions. In the external field, before the failure of the negotiations with Bolivia to conclude the Treaty of Friendship and Alliance that defended the independence and territorial integrity of Peru and the existence of conspiracies of his enemy General Andrés de Santa Cruz developed in Cusco and Arequipa; they took to the president of the Republic to request to the Congress extraordinary faculties to declare the war and to invade this country.

From then until January 4, 1832, there was a truce with the neighboring country embodied in the treaties of Tiquina, Arequipa and Chuquisaca, which raised the compliance in favor of the principle of non-intervention, the immediate termination of all seditious activity, the provisional recognition of border limits between the former High and Low Peru, the recognition of reciprocal rights between both countries. Internally, the congress wanted to stop the political aspirations of Gamarra by limiting the presence of Spaniards and Chileans in their military environment. In this way, the law of September 25, 1831, indicated that the staff and army officers should be composed by Peruvians and victors of Junín and Ayacucho.

While the president was out of Lima, he was replaced by Antonio Gutiérrez de La Fuente who committed a series of arbitrary acts during his administration until his deportation by Gamarra. Very recurrent institution in the nineteenth century among the political class, especially as in this case, if the candidates for the two senior executive positions were appointed by the Congress without considering the empathy between them. His absence did not prevent in 1832 the Council of State sent to the Chamber of Deputies a list of constitutional violations committed by the Executive where the acts committed by the vice president before his exile were found. Nor did it prevent the president of the Chamber of Deputies, Francisco de Paula Gonzales Vigil, from pronouncing his famous phrase: I must accuse, I accuse; directed against the president Agustín Gamarra, but that in fact included the arbitrariness of his exvicepresidente and the critics to the administrative acts committed by the ministers of the regime.

VII. THE NATIONAL CONVENTION AND THE CONSTITUTION OF 1834

Under the leadership of Gonzales Vigil was installed the National Convention that approved the law that ordered the election of the provisional president while the constitutional reform was concluded, object of the call. In this process of political consolidation, Jamanca claims the figure of this republican:

"... capable of sacrificing his life in order to give himself up to the defense of the public good. Public spirit, ethics, anti-corruption, constitutionalism are the recurring themes. His life and work are a clear example of what the republican tradition represents in Peru "(Jamanca, 2015, 150).

Consolidation that also heard the voices of liberals like Manuel Lorenzo Vidaurre, who before the power of the military caudillo wanted to limit his interference in the politics of the incipient republic, without noticing that the problem was structural and not mediatic:

"A military man can never be elected president of the republic, if he is the one who concludes his term. In twelve periods the president can not be re-elected. The barracked troops can never be more than a quarter of the disciplined militias "(Vidaurre, 1998, 371)

The Constitution gradually became the instrument to regulate the use of public force:

"... Peru is awaiting the fate of a newly conquered people, if the plan is carried out. We can already say that we are with garrisons. The pictures are filled, the cams are made, and the army is increased, without respect to the law. There is no money that reaches the expenses of marches and countermarches "(Pareja, 1944, p 69).

Months after the congress was installed, the incorporation of Javier Luna Pizarro was gravitating in the election of the chief executive, since he inclined the appointment to a candidate without pretensions of power and nothing authoritarian embodied in Luis José de Orbegoso, ex-Count of Olmos, who defeated the official general candidate Pedro Bermúdez. Measure that could not prevent the permanent harassment of the caudillos to the precarious system, led by Bermudez himself and months later by Felipe Santiago Salaverry. The one who was named Provisional Supreme Chief led a new coup on January 3, 1834, which was backed by the prefects of Cuzco, Puno and Ayacucho. The Convention was closed after two companies from the Piquiza battalion took over the premises where it operated. Legislative members moved to Callao where support for General Bermúdez faded and the navy closed ranks to illegality. Once again in Lima on February 13, the Convention resumed its functions in support of Orbegoso and declared Bermúdez's government acts null and void.

On June 11, the new Constitution was promulgated and sworn. One of the key points was the return for the supranational interest in the territorial scope, although the alternative of the Bolivarian Federation had had a bad impression for the nationalism. Luna Pizarro came to the conviction that due to historical circumstances the link with Upper Peru should be maintained, because she believed that:

"In the federation, Bolivia will meet Peru, the department of La Paz will cede to form the State of the Center, Tacna will be the capital of the Confederation ..." (Távara, 1951, p. 62).

Intention that was reflected in Article 1 of the Constitution of 1834 by omitting the clause that prevented any kind of limitation by annexing us to another State such as Bolivia:

"The Peruvian nation is independent and can not be patrimony of any person or family", tacitly suppressing the considered part that stated: "... nor will admit with another Union State or federation that opposes its independence" [Article 2 of the Constitution of 1828].

In the internal aspect, the principle of decentralization that resided in the Departmental Boards disappeared. For the designation of the Prefects and Subprefects, the candidates were proposed through a list of six people by the polling stations in each regional demarcation to the President of the Republic, who appointed them. The granting of citizenship resumed the age of majority at 21, having been born in the territory or being the son of a national father and mother, a Catholic, not being broken. The Chamber of Deputies reserved the election of the judges of first instance suggested by the lists of the electoral colleges. As for the vacancy of the members of the Superior Court, it was based on the list drawn up by the magistrates themselves and sent by the electoral college to the Senate. The election of the positions for the Supreme Court depended on a list proposed by said school, which was seen by the Congress in plenary. The same procedure was applied for the appointment for the first time for the conformation of the Supreme Council of War, which is an important milestone when incorporating military justice within the Rule of Law.

As for the Executive, the presidential reelection was proposed leaving a mandate, discarding the immediate modality of 1828. In the order of succession of power, the figure of the vice president of the Republic disappeared and, in his place, and temporarily assumed the direction of the country the president of the Council of State. This institution was composed of two councilors for each department and may or not be a member of the Senate Chamber and were elected by Congress.

In cases of political instability, the President of the Republic was prohibited from using the National Guard outside its provincial limits except for sedition or external aggression. The military force was also a matter of reorganization of state control, restricting the number of effective seats as long as there were no vacancies.

Another control was carried out by the congressional body that designated the land and sea contingents, giving its approval for the appointment of generals, colonels and ship captains, direct faculty that had held the Executive. Finally, the constitutional charter ordered the loss of the civil rights of the ruler who gave coup, as well as the declaration of nullity of their actions, also pointing out the disobedience of society to any authority that did not count on the legitimacy consecrated in the elections. The right of claim of any individual before Congress or the Executive was established for alleged constitutional violation that violated their rights. Instrument of control that added to the called Judgment of Residence coming from the virreinato, according to which, all civil servant of the administration was subject to the control of the State at the end of his position, without which he was unable to exercise another.

VII. FROM THE FEDERATION TO THE PERU-BOLIVIAN CONFEDERATION

The supranational interest of the Congress aroused the nationalism of the young general Felipe Santiago Salaverry, then brigadier of General Luis José de Orbegoso, president of the Republic, leading a coup d'état on February 22, 1835 that elevated him as Supreme Chief, at the age of 29 years. The need to recover the capital demanded the deposed president to require the help of General Andres de Santa Cruz, to defeat the insurgent for which the Treaty of Relief was held on June 15 of that year, through which Bolivia would provide an army to pacify the country. However, the scope of the legal instrument went beyond pacification by conforming assemblies in the south and north that would decide the bases of the Peru-Bolivian Confederation under the leadership of Santa Cruz.

Gamarra thought that the Bolivian presence after the signing of the treaty was understood as an invasion of the national territory, which caused the army factions close to him to confront the Santa Cruz army; process that culminated with the defeat of the Cuzco leader and his subsequent expatriation. With the panorama clear, Santa Cruz initiated his proposal of form of government that included the presence of Federated States.

In Sicuani, the representatives of the southern departments were summoned, a total of 23, on March 16, 1836. Under the presidency of Nicolás de Piérola, this assembly declared the birth of the Peruvian Southern State. Months later, according to the law of 1834, the same thing happened in the north, with the representation of the departments of Amazonas, La Libertad, Junín and Lima meeting in Huaura. The assembly chaired by Evaristo Gómez Sánchez, on August 11, 1836, created the birth of the Nor-Peruvian State, accepting Orbegoso as its President, recognizing the existence of the Southern Peruvian State and granting powers to Santa Cruz as Protector. This did not deny the existence of an opposition to the articulation with the south, of which it did not find a greater link. The legislative bodies of both States agreed with the integration of the State of Bolivia the creation of the Peru-Bolivian Confederation, designating General Santa Cruz as its Protector. Regime that had its legal basis in Treaty of

Confederation signed in 1837 during the Congress of plenipotentiaries convened in the city of Tacna:

"This is how the Peruvian family dislocated without consulting the will; thus the foreign tyranny to the constitutional regime happened and thus the old Republic disappeared, since the most abominable betrayal destroyed their institutions "(Dancuart, 1901, Volume IV, p. 127).

However, this treaty was not perfected due to the absence of the exchange of ratifications, which later led to the same regime declaring it insubstantiated. This version of the federal regime enjoyed a strong, autocratic government that promoted the formation of an oligarchy, an instrument that guaranteed the institutional continuity of the region.

The legislature continued to be bicameral, but with variations in membership and functions. The Chamber of Senators made up of a total of 15 members, at the rate of five representatives, was appointed by each State, for which the state electoral colleges proposed lists to the Head of the Confederation, who appointed them.

The Senators enjoyed the position for life in comparisson to the censors of the Constitution of 1826, except by court sentence for infamous penalty. The House of Representatives conformed by 21 members, seven of which belonged to each State. Their respective electoral entities sent their lists to the General Congress of the Confederation which finally elected them. The mandate was six years and was renewed by thirds. This central Congress met every two years, being able to meet in any member state. Their sessions lasted up to fifty days with the possibility of extension, according to the gravity of the affairs of the country and at the discretion of the Protector.

The design of the organs was subject to the consolidation of the Central Congress and the convocation of the Constitutional Legislative that gave the fundamental law of the country. With a duration of 10 years, the Protector of the Peru-Bolivian Confederation was the highest representative of the Executive Branch and may be re-elected unless he suffered sanction from the Senate that promotes his dismissal.
Of the candidates nominated by double triples of the state congresses, the central legislature appointed the Protector what in fact was not fulfilled with Santa Cruz, who was declared as such by the assemblies of Sicuani and Huaura, conferring broad powers. He was head of the Central Administration, head of the military force, appointed the magistrates of the three States according to the lists presented by their respective senates. In the absence of the Protector, the Ministers of State meeting in council and under the leadership of the oldest ruled temporarily. On the same date they called a general election to choose the next protector.

Opposition to the march of the Bolivian Peru Confederation aroused the rejection of the inhabitants of the departments of Huaylas and La Libertad, who opposed in 1838 the continuity of Santa Cruz, proposing the nullity of administrative acts and proclaiming the independence of the integrity of the territory. Orbegoso was commissioned to carry forward these proposals, as president of the Nor Peruvian State. This exhibition opened the possibility of undermining the political project of Santa Cruz, since gradually the Peruvian territorial demarcations were returning to the previous state before the confederation, only that this time they were involved in the presence of two foreign armies: Bolivians and Chileans.

This conjuncture provoked consensual demonstrations that sought to recover the legitimacy in the management of power. Faced with the debacle of the Santa Cruz regime, notable people of Lima agreed to retake the Council of State, appointing Manuel Salazar and Baquíjano as its president and entrusting Agustín Gamarra with the direction of the Executive Power to rebuild the country.

The situation demanded to put an end to the backwardness of the previous regime, but also, as the provisional president of Peru, to call elections for a new national representation. The Board of Directors called the Police Commission under the presidency of Manuel Bartolomé Ferreyros, Agustín Guillermo Charún and Lucas Pellicer. In the city of Huancayo, the 70 representatives in the first act ratified the President of the Republic as provisional agent, granting him honors according to his high office.

The constituents concluded that the new Charter should gather the experience of the events of the last decade that demanded the leadership of a strong government and that were not alien to the victorious military leader. Legislators such as cleric Agustín Guillermo Charún (Cañete) and Bernardo Soffía (Lima), who took the profile of the provisional president as their model, would be in charge of this. Orbegoso was declared a traitor to the country, Santa Cruz, main enemy of Peru, in the same way the military Guillermo Miller, Jose de la Riva Agüero, Blas Sardinia, among others were removed from the ranks. [El Comercio, October 29, 1839]. The deprivation of political rights against the 23 representatives of the Assembly of Sicuani and the 20 of Huaura was also decreed.

CHAPTER THREE

The return of nationalism

I. THE LETTER OF 1839 AND THE ANARCHY

The drafting of the draft of the Charter of 1839 allows us to appreciate the great influence of Benjamin Constant in the legislative drafting:

"In our current societies, the birth in the country and the maturity of age are not enough to confer on men the qualities required for the exercise of citizenship rights: Those whom the indigence maintains in a perpetual dependence and condemnation to daily work they have no greater illustration than children about public affairs, nor do they have greater interest than foreigners in a national prosperity whose elements they do not know and in whose benefits they only participate directly. " (Constant, 1970 p. 153).

The Constitution was promulgated on November 10, the Legislature transformed into ordinary Congress was dedicated to order the presidential election in accordance with the law of November 29, 1839, in which the acting president participated, who was elected in January of the following year. The new political legal order included the prohibition of any treaty that would endanger the independence of the country, which implicitly excluded proposals for regional integration in South America. Variations were introduced in the granting of nationality, regarding the children of a Peruvian father or mother there were two conditions: that the parents were in the service of the Peruvian nation and that those born were registered in the civil registry of Lima.

On the other hand, for the naturalization of foreigners, it was specified that it was granted for: having served in the army or the navy, being useful to the prosperity of the country, exercising an art or industry, having a four-year residency (previously of two) or have contracted marriage with Peruvians. The Spaniards were left to express their domicile in the country through their registration in the civil registry. The political capacity or citizenship was granted to every Peruvian, national or naturalized, married, retaking the majority at age 25, being literate - requirement of which mestizos and Indians were exempt until 1844- and paying some contribution. Ability that could be lost by sentence of infamous punishment, naturalization in another State, having accepted the grace of another nation without the consent of Congress, fraudulent bankruptcy declared judicially, taking religious vows of closure or infringing the peace with weapons against the constituted authority.

The Legislative Power was organized in a bicameral manner, to be a deputy it was established 30 years and 40 years for senator, also had to enjoy an income which was increased in the second charge and residence was required according to the place they represented. With a mandate of six years, the deputies were renewed by thirds every two years, and in the case of Senators with a period of eight years, by halves. They were granted immunity from not being prosecuted for debt or civilly sued.

This power of the State had to meet every two years either for the election of the President of the Republic, declare his vacancy, elect state councilors, declare war, grant extraordinary powers to the Head of State with charge to inform about what was acted upon. The election of the head of the Executive began in the electoral colleges that sent to the Legislative the minutes of the elections, this one called for a second election proclaiming finally a winner. The mandate was extended from four to six years, with re-election possible after a period. The political responsibility of the management was carried out at the end of the exercise of power through the Residence Trial.

The experience with Bolivia demanded that any attempt to unite or confederate be a cause for vacancy. The order of priority in the succession of presidential command fell to the members of the Council of State: first, its president, the first vice president and finally the second president. The events of 1842 put this system to the test; After the substitution of the person who previously held the position, it could not always be recovered immediately. The powers granted to the President of the Republic were so broad that it allowed him to have interference in the appointments, as well as in the removals of the magistrates, with the approval of the Council of State in the case of superior and supreme members. In addition to the above requirements, the age to be a minister in any of the four administrations was raised to 40 years. It was mandatory the ministerial endorsement to give validity to the presidential acts, sharing the political responsibility.

The Council of State was strengthened by holding powers previously conferred by Congress such as the granting of extraordinary powers to the Executive, however, its conformation ceased to respond to the departmental link granted by the previous Constitution. Its members continued to be elected by the Legislature inside or outside it and were renewed by half every two years. A quota was established for its fifteen members, where the military and ecclesiastics could not surpass three representations respectively. Their agreements gravitated on the operation of the state administration, collaboration with the chambers in the formulation of bills of their initiative and oversight in the observance of the constitution and laws. It replaced the Congress when it was in recess and had the faculty to summon it extraordinarily.

The Charter of 1839 maintained the slavery by rocignizing as Peruvians by birth only free men born in national territory, a statement that contradicted the statement that no one was born a slave in Peru. As for the armed forces, we wanted to establish a hierarchy and a number in the military commands: a great marshal, three generals of division, six of brigade, a vice admiral and a rear admiral, effective positions that should be according to potential vacancies to be produced. However, the most important thing was to emphasize the character of these forces subordinated to obedience and non-deliberation in front of the other civil state authorities and compliance with the Constitution and laws. In the internal regime, the municipalities were suppressed and in their replacement the prefects and police mayors (and in some cases the trustees) were in charge. The latter with executive, judicial and administrative powers.

The constitutional reform was rigidly established with five moments for its reading and debate, after which it was passed to the meeting of the two chambers to elaborate the substitute project, with which it was practically impossible to accept an amendment. The Constitution was approved and allowed a better organization of the Executive by lengthening the mandate to six years, providing the Supreme Court the right of initiative for a better administration of justice and a more leading role of the State Council.

As we have argued before, culturally, before the disappearance of the lands of curacazgo, the Gamarrista regime protected the settlers who took advantage of the land, making use of the method of allocation and composition of land, which recognized occupation as a way of acquisition, Figure that would be ratified in the law of May 24, 1845 also incorporating foreigners as beneficiaries. Thus, the authority acted in a paternal way in the new towns, making the process to dispose of the land was of the administration and therefore of government of the day. The death of Marshal Agustín Gamarra in the battle of Ingavi, put to the test the principle of authority of the Charter because it was not possible for the order to rest only in one person but in the institutions that reflected the concurrence of wills, otherwise they ended for being nominal.

The political stability also favored a new debate led by Bartolomé Herrera Vélez, considered as the founder of the political class of the mid-nineteenth century, whose members seconded the teachings of his teacher and the brothers José and Pedro Gálvez Egúsquiza. Born in Lima in 1808, a student of the Real Convictorio de San Carlos and later ordained a priest, he turned his pastoral work as a member of the Catholic Church as a parish priest carrying his mission to the educational level as rector of his Alma Mater in 1842. and the instability that the country was going through led him to turn away from the revolutionary Frenchness that had impregnated the political culture of that time.
Works such as those of Joseph Marie, Count de Maistre, François Guizot and Donoso Cortés, Marquis of Valdegamas influenced the current model of democracy that demanded the desired order in response to the present debacle. It was Guizot (1831), a representative of the liberal doctrine who, along with Benjamin Constant, chose to endorse the constitutional monarchy in France, orienting himself to raise the qualification of the electorate, through the selection of owners of the ruling bourgeoisie and the organization of political forces. Opposed to the expanded vote, he proposed to his nationals that they enrich themselves to later count on the granting of citizenship.

The first reflection of Herrera is found in the prayer during the funerals held on January 4, 1842 in the Church of the Cathedral of Lima for the soul of S.E. the

Jeneralísimo (sic) President of the Republic D. Agustín Gamarra pronounced the Dr. D. Bartolomé Herrera, Priest and Vicar of Lurín:

"After the strong shock suffered by our society to dismember the vast monarchy that was part, it was inevitable that they experienced confusion and misfortune, to set the new center of order, the authority that should replace the Spanish Sovereign. But once established this authority, distributed political powers; fixed the guarantees of citizens, greeted the young republic for the kingdoms of Europe who saw full of hope their opulence and their charms, Why do we experience so much evil? Why have we been sinking into an abyss? How has this people rich in talents, in value and in all kinds of resources, been able to suffer the last humiliation of seeing their territory desecrated, and defeated their army by that of a state, which should shudder to contemplate our power from afar? Let us judge gentlemen, with impartiality and in us we will find the cause of our affront. " (Herrera, 1929-1930, pp. 14-15).

From the Convictorio de San Carlos his work was fertile, convinced that the formation of a new generation of politicians was necessary:

"shortly, before eight years, a new generation will leave San Carlos to blind the source of tears that has flooded the Republic (Pareja, 1944, p.107).

Circumstances demanded the response to the uncertainty and improvisation of which the ephemeral regimes had been subjected. The training received by the intellectuals compelled them to defend above all things the country as the highest value of society and this would only be achieved through the exercise of the Powers of the State and the development of freedoms that attended the person's life same to which was added the development and progress that we would experience in the middle of the 19th century.

Juan Donoso Cortés argued that the political model should be regulated by the invocation of justice and the application of the sovereignty of intelligence. Justice that was imperative and served as a guarantee to the exercise of the proclaimed and limited rights. Sovereignty, that rescued from the doctrinal liberals the requisites for this faculty, but where the most capable could carry out the divine will, the providentialism. By having them the possibility of leisure could be illustrated and have a better disposition to influence political destinations. A look at the development of Peruvian political thought from Bartolomé Herrera can also lead us to the reflection of approaches in the second and third decade of the twentieth century with the aptitude or the government of the capable or capable, as Luis Echecopar would say, in 1931.

Meanwhile in politics, the death of President Gamarra caused anarchy that was not spontaneous and led to the emergence of caudillos, who monopolized the political life of the country: Francisco Vidal, Manuel Vivanco Ignacio, Juan Crisostomo Torrico, Antonio Gutierrez de La Source, Ramón Castilla and Domingo Nieto. The adherents and alliances allowed them to concentrate the forces that displaced their contender. From this succession we can observe towards 1843, the leadership in the north central zone of Francisco Vidal and especially in Arequipa with Vivanco, each one of them maintained from his point of view that the establishment of a congress would restore institutionality, hence the importance to propitiate the elections as soon as possible the failure of Vivanco in the battle of Carmen Alto, which allowed the restitution of the Council of State in charge of the prefect of Lima Domingo Elías, who had the support of Ramón Castilla. Castilla, virtual winner of the presidential elections, traveled to Arequipa to defeat the supporters of Vivanco, restoring the unitary management of the central power.

In June the Congress was constituted in Lima, which did not accept limitations and that same month it was declared in ordinary legislature. Of these inspection processes between the organs of power, the first resignation of a minister arose at the request of the Congress. The deputy for Ica Pedro de la Quintana, based on the assertion that the congress represented the popular will asserted the proposal of the sovereignty of Parliament, which could force the resignation of a minister on passing the power of accusation, as constitutionally both the attribution of the removal and the appointment were of the President of the Republic. Manuel del Río, minister of finance of the regime suffered the inclemencies of personal intrigues, citing criticism for his management in the ministry. Although the motion that was approved by a large majority in the Chamber of Deputies did not have the same effect in the Senate. The resignation of Del Rio accepted by Castilla, although meant the strengthening of the Legislative in the balance of forces, did not imply the questioning of the presidential figure, linked to the imprisonment or exile of politicians opposed to previous regimes.

On the other hand, the caudillo was conscious of maintaining order, as claimed as a source of authority and of the State itself, that would promote the political stability possible for economic changes. While it is true that the President of the Republic ceded positions, this did not prevent him from having adherents to the interior of the Legislative and to seek the legitimacy of governmental acts. The transfer of command from Ramón Castilla to Rufino Echenique made us perceive an institutional stability not only in the Executive but in the State that left behind the anarchic image. For its part, the Legislative was called to address other issues of state and social regulation as stipulated by the corresponding decree of April 30, 1851: the sanction of civil codes and procedures, ratification of the law of elections, the establishment of the municipalities, the reconsideration of the law of military conscription, the complement of the consolidation of the internal debt that included the previous one of the independence, the existence of the currency of low law that circulates, the exoneration of the payment of patents to the artisans, the state of public income, the commerce regulations and the events in Arequipa.

The return to stability motivated the Congress to establish, by law of October 5, 1845, a new codifying commission for the drafting of the civil code. Four years later the review commission was appointed and in 1851, the definitive commission. In this sequence we note both the participation of liberals and conservatives, who in their way expressed their concerns in legal institutions. The pressure of the government led to two promulgations, the one of Ramón Castilla with an unfinished code and the definitive one during Rufino Echenique's mandate on July 28, 1852. This marked the beginning of the systematized substitution of the Spanish legislation in force in the civil sphere by a national one, a process that would gradually be applied in the other subjects based on more integrated texts.

Although the interest to strengthen the State was appreciated during Echenique's term, we observed a slowness in the solution of priority issues in the social field. However, the crucial issue of the regime was the payment in the consolidation of the internal debt that in spite of total figures estimated during the previous regime, this one was surpassed by four times said amount, causing borders of scandal and waste of the state resources. This was the trigger to generate the uprising of General Castilla, who surrounded by doctrinaire liberals like the Gálvez brothers took advantage of the situation to draft the decrees that made possible the elimination of the contribution of indigenous people and slavery.

To the income generated by the exploitation of guano was added the presence of the so-called second liberalism, whose representatives in addressing social issues, under the premise of the claim, had difficulties in applying this theory to the indigenous case. The prejudice of not considering it as an economic agent was retained, which was far from a true analysis of the situation of the city and its articulation with the State. During December 5, 1854, Ramón Castilla issued decrees in the city of Huancayo, which allowed abolishing the contribution of the Indians and slavery, both colonial backwardness. For this, he had the help of the liberals: the Minister of Worship, Justice and Finance, Manuel Toribio Ureta; and, from the Minister of Government, Foreign Affairs and War, Pedro José Gálvez Egúsquiza. These changes to the formation of society were the beginning of the process of adapting a medium that still retained its corporate ties, maintaining the domain of the interests of the elites over the social forces that emerged before the authority of the state apparatus.

On the other hand, it was expected that the consolidation of the debt would have created a new social group interested in strengthening the country and not the deployment of a level of corruption little known until then. In political terms, the coup against Echenique shows us a recomposition of the Congress that would lead to the formation of the National Convention of Deputies.

II. THE CONSTITUTION OF 1856 AND THE SECOND LIBERAL WAVE

By decree of February 5, 1855, the Liberator and Provisional President Ramón Castilla convened a National Convention of Deputies, elected for the first time by direct and universal suffrage, excluding the requirements of the vote census, as well as the politicians of the Echenique government. This process of suffrage was carried out through the municipalities counting on the civil registry, fruit of which we find for the period 1855 to 1857: 85 holders and 64 substitutes. Again the forces of the liberals and conservatives stood out, that unlike the first decades were more doctrinaire. With 72 deputies, the Legislature was installed on July 14, 1855 and among its first acts ratified Castilla as Provisional President of the Republic, in recognition of the leadership of this leader who wanted to institutionalize the country. This Legislature appointed the members of the Constitution Committee for the drafting of the new Charter. It was necessary to resume the operation of the State considering the consequences of the political events that took place.

The liberals, under the personality of their leader José Gálvez Egúsquiza, insisted on the protagonism of the person in society and under the protection of the State. This was the first fact that characterized Gálvez, opposed to the return of the old order, perceiving him as a just man within an environment that had been prone to tolerate abuses to the detriment of all, until then. Our character was in favor of reforming the army, regardless of the informal and improvised, and those undefined military, that despite having a degree, they lacked placement. That is why he was convinced that before generating a greater number of troops, first the number of jobs needed must be analyzed. In its design, the Constitution of 1856 emphasized that after the nation and religion, the rights and freedoms were expressed under the name of individual guarantees. Whereas, their predecessors had given priority to the organization of the State.

It placed the Constitution as the supreme norm against the norm:

"Art. 10.- Any law is null and void as soon as it opposes the Constitution. The acts of those who usurp public functions and the jobs conferred without the requirements prescribed by the Constitution and the laws are also null. " (García Belaunde, 2016, p.316)

On the other hand, the adoption of equality before the law, in all its effects, posed the incompatibility with the existence of privileges especially ecclesiastical and military, considered as lags of a corporate society that still maintained its privileges, which occurred with the validity of the tithes and firstfruits. Due to the strong Catholic roots and their relationship with the State, it was not possible to accept Catholic interference, as before. As for the military aspect, the controversy went further and came to question the convenience of the existence of the army.

Ignacio Escudero, deputy for Piura, considered that the permanent armies could be substituted with the armed citizens, since they lived in leisure, being able to use this force in the industry. Pedro Gálvez refuted the comment stating the need for army maintenance, given the dangers of fragile external and internal instability. However, the acceptance did not deny that the Congress had greater interference in military promotions, including then from a senior graduate in the army and captain of a corvette in the navy, technical positions that obey more the criteria of the institutes.

The defense of the individual led to the prohibition of the death penalty, since society lacked that right, considering human life inviolable. As for political matters, the issue of amnesty was approved, and it was established that the Executive lacked the power to suspend constitutional guarantees.

José Gabriel Gálvez Egúsquiza, leader of doctrinaire liberalism in Peru.
National Museum of Chile

This section also promoted the pretension to avoid the concentration of power in one of the state organs, hence the predominance of the role of the Executive would soon be questioned. For the liberals it was necessary to diminish the functions of this entity and its subsequent transfer to the Legislative, indirectly avoiding the concentration of power. For this, the role of decentralization was also appealed through the departmental boards, which would influence the municipalities and the territorial organization of the country.

The creation of the Council of Ministers with which the legislators departed from the American liberal model. Institution that limited the presidential activity by emphasizing the idea of the endorsement and that caused the disappearance of the State Council. Progressively this support body of the Chief Executive, from December 5, 1857 tried to channel the presidential impetus through the administrative coordination of the different items that concur in this management.

On the other hand, the Legislative Branch reorganized the functions of the Public Ministry with the creation of the figure of the National Prosecutor, who would be responsible for compliance with the laws. The impossibility of observing the new Charter led to a series of tensions revealed in its recognition and acceptance to the point that it was not the sympathy of the different regions of the country.

From Arequipa there was a movement that refused to swear to the Constitution and that again enlisted Manuel de Vivanco, with the support of social forces from other departments. The movement concluded in Callao where the president of the Republic, although he beat the southern military man, perceived the disagreement over the character that the State had taken. The leadership of the conventional ones was determining to approve a norm against the critics coming from publications or communications against his institution, which was counterproductive to go against the precept of the freedom of opinion and the law of the press. In the month of November of 1856, a new incident served to measure the political forces of the State. Army commander Pablo Arguedas, a subordinate of General Pedro Diez Canseco (brother-in-law of Castile), entered with a detachment of soldiers and dissolved the National Convention.

The operation of the Convention, as the government's controlling entity, ended up preventing further changes. Its members had insisted on holding the right to scrutiny of the upcoming elections for the Executive in order to maintain political leadership. Here was the first cut of doctrinaire liberalism. Pedro and José Gálvez, sons of Cajamarca, and Liberals were in favor of the expansion of rights, the abolition of the death penalty and the granting of the vote to the indigenous people. For Herrera, the Indian, being illiterate, could not be considered capable of integrating the electorate of that time; even more so when this extension suggested the possibility of buying their votes; nevertheless, the Andean settlers paid taxes and under the French argument that the one who pays votes, their claim was reasonable.

Herrera's theory reconciled the capacity referred to as a prerequisite sine qua non with morality, honesty and identity manifested as patriotism. This exclusion did not mean to fail to recognize the contribution of the autochthonous as the Incas, who by their order and unity made the evangelization and catechization enterprise feasible, taking the gospel to the known lands. The Spanish tradition, on the other hand, provided unity, stability and order. Of these values, order represented the priority theme that he wanted to translate into a political project.

We owe it to the work of the Convictorio de San Carlos, bastion of the conservatives, the recent Colegio Nuestra Señora de Guadalupe was added, founded by Gálvez himself together with Domingo Elías and Juan Rodríguez. They were joined by: the Cisneros, Carrillo, Althaus, Colonel Juan Espinosa, author of the Dictionary for the people or José Simeón Tejeda and were produced from the parliamentary precincts, whether the National Convention of 1855, the Congresses of 1858 and 1860 or from the press. Debates related to natural rights, the secular school, State control over the Church and the Army, decentralization and even the death penalty where José Gálvez Egúsquiza, included in the Constitution of 1856 in his article 16: Human life is inviolable; the law can not impose the death penalty (García Belaunde, 2016, 316).

Statement that subject of modification in the Congress of 1860 where Herrera argued that the right to impose penalties came from the sovereign power, which ultimately derived from the same God. Until his death in the Combat of May 2, 1866, Gálvez was the icon of liberalism whose changes were suggestive, and others advanced in the mid-nineteenth century.

III. THE CONSTITUTION OF 1860, THE LONGEST

The liberal attitude had created antibodies in the different social groups, hence the protest for the dissolution of the Convention had no greater reception because it benefited different entities that expected the vindication of their rights violated and gave the government the opportunity to act freely. After the dissolution of the National Convention, by decree of November of 1857 issued by the Council of Ministers, the convocation was made for president and vice president of the Republic, as well as for the members of the Legislative.

On August 12, 1858, the Extraordinary Congress met, granting Ramón Castilla y Marquesado and Juan Manuel del Mar the ownership of the positions they held provisionally. Domestic affairs such as the uprising in Ayacucho, and the situation with Ecuador in the external panorama, motivated the congressman, through the law of May 24, 1859, to declare his recess so as not to hinder the work of the Head of State, however, he agreed to mutually resume his duties on the following July 28. This agreement was considered by the President of the Republic as unconstitutional because only he had to make the call. Situation that allowed Castilla to call elections for the ordinary Congress of 1860. During the process of the preparatory meetings, Pio Benigno Meza, deputy for La Convención, denounced irregularities such as the presentation of up to 4 candidates for the same seat and the incorporation of Bartolomé Herrera as representative of Jauja, according to that incompatible with his new condition as bishop. Argument that did not prosper because it was considered that the constitutional election was prior to the episcopal appointment.

On the installation date, which gathered 120 incumbents and 4 deputies, Rep. Meza proposed that a lottery be drawn up to form the two chambers, an approach that was suspended, given that days later it would be decided whether Congress would act with ordinary faculties, that is, constituted through its two Chambers or, on the contrary, it would be a constituent with powers to reform the current Constitution, after which it would be dissolved. In fact, this Legislative functioned with both characteristics, first decided to reform and later elected 36 members to become Senators, while the rest would remain as Deputies, which formed the ordinary Congress. The responsibility of the president of the Republic was limited, being able to be accused during his mandate for the crimes of treason, change the form of government, dissolve the

Congress or prevent their meeting. On the other hand, said president was obliged to give an account to the Legislative of the governmental acts at the conclusion of his administration. The spirit of this new Constitution was aimed at reducing the role of the government in front of a Congress that recovered the bicamerality.

We must indicate the intention to propose a special modality for this last conformation based on the corporatism of the different professions. During the recess of the Legislative, the Permanent Commission was established in the Charter, whose legislative and administrative powers came from the previous Council of State and which had already worked in Peru in 1829, as we saw. Although the purpose of its attributions was to limit the arbitrariness of the government, its faculties were stipulated so extensively that they led to its suppression years later. The issue of presidential reelection was developed under fallacious criteria. On the one hand, it was argued that if the president had made a good government it was fair that he should be re-elected. The continuity in power should be given as an opportunity for the president to be worthy of it. Criteria that were not in function of the State but of the character that occupied the position, since previous experiences already had demonstrated the particular interest to perpetuate themselves in the position.

On the other hand, disappeared the figure of the Prosecutor of the Nation being replaced by two prosecutors appointed by the Supreme Court, being retaken in 1979 with the nascent Public Ministry. Although there was a suppression of the amovility of the magistrates' jobs, on the part of the Executive, this position did not mean that their independence was favored, since it was not considered any interference in the electoral controversies. We could point out that, as a counterpart, initiative was recognized in bills on legal matters. The death penalty was reinstated by refuting the thesis of the inviolability of life by the attribution that the State had of the punitive monopoly based on power, since, being sovereign, its quality came from God himself. This penalty was applied only for qualified homicide. The phenomenon of militarism was also the subject of the legislators, who recognized the role of the military force to the detriment of the military, but this did not exclude the establishment of limits in the exercise of their functions. The military force could not be deliberative, it had to comply with the law and the civil power that embodied the nation. In other words, it wanted to subordinate constitutionally especially the army since it was part of the State itself. The Legislature diminished its interference in military promotions by counting from the degrees of captain in the navy and colonel effective, as well as general, which established a bond of obedience according to law. Another way to limit their actions was to question the recruitment of individuals to the army, carried out through the cam or arbitrary detention, whose objective was the forced incorporation of people. Feel that it was picked up in the second part of Article 123 of the Constitution of 1860.

As for the individual, the legislators continued with the abolition of the ecclesiastical jurisdiction and that had provoked the rejection of certain regions when swearing in the previous Constitution because it was considered in addition that the ecclesiastical connections favored the capitals and benefits of the priests of all the country, being its only source of income. On the contrary, the military jurisdiction that had proved to be an entity that preserved the uses of pre-independent society was maintained. Although the achievements of the previous Charter referring to individual guarantees such as the legal protection of honor and life against all useless and unjust aggression were suppressed, as well as the principle that the norm was not retroactive, others such as: guarantee that no one can be detained without a court order and must be made available to the judge within 24 hours after the fact; the consideration that contributions were established only in proportion to the taxpayer and their destination was for public services; the equality of civil rights for foreigners and nationals and the possibility of filing popular action against constitutional infringements. The granting of Peruvian citizenship was restricted only to those born in the national territory and abroad for those children of a Peruvian father and mother.

The law of elections of April 1861 resumed indirect suffrage, alleging that the country lacked education and civic preparation, in response to the National Convention, in the same way, Congress reserved the qualification of the electoral acts, the cameras being the calls to contemplate the procedural aspects. The new charter was promulgated on November 13, 1860 and two days later the Congress closed its sessions. Subsequently, a series of changes took place, this Charter having partial reforms, which began with the law of August 31, 1874, which abolished the Permanent Commission. Later, another innovation was the law of September 10, 1887 that allowed the compatibility of positions of congressman with that of Minister of State, with the permission of his House, in the parliamentary style and that continues in force.

Bartolomé Herrera as deputy, president of the Chamber of Deputies, president of the Senate and president of the Congress presented his draft Constitution that combined the intellectuality with parliamentary practices developed before the views found by the liberal character of the Constitution of 1856. He stressed first the relations with the Catholic Church, which had been affected by the Charter of 1856 by abolishing the ecclesiastical jurisdiction for which it demanded its restoration, as well as the tithes and the dead hand regime.

The granting of citizenship was granted to those over 21, married or widowed, but lost due to lack of intelligence (according to the loss of capacity due to prodigality stipulated by the Civil Code of 1852, article 16 and following (Civil Code , 1870, 15), lack of freedom or those who do not have the financial means to subsist, established that the State guaranteed freedom and property provided they did not attempt against religion, public order and the rights of third parties.

The presence of elected members of a group of political forces represents the novelty in the congressional composition, which, unlike the deputies, would be selective in representing the state and social institutions in the Upper House: "Thus, the Senate consisted of 30 members, three for each of the following ten careers: political career (Ministers of State or Plenipotentiaries, Prefects, Senior Officials of the Ministries), Finance (senior employees of that branch or postal), of the Magistracy (Members of the Supreme or of the Superior Courts), ecclesiastical (Bishops, canons or dignities), of the Army and Navy (from Coronel up); parliamentary (which had been elected three times deputies or concurred to three legislatures), scientific professions (which included those who taught for more than twenty years); to the owners (the miners or farmers) to the merchants and capitalists, with capital greater than 200,000 pesos "(Pareja, 1944, 114)

Corporate mode of organization that will have a better development in the version of Victor Andres Belaunde and in the Constitution of 1933, but being oriented to the organizations of the society, of a guild character previously incrited that to the state ones. As for the functions developed by this collegiate, they were limited specifically to those of a municipal nature and to the celebration of international treaties and concordats, the general military promotions of the army and admiral in the navy, exceptionally electing the President of the Republic. As for the Legislative Executive relationship, the bill granted the Presidential character to the Constitution by providing the Head of State with the appointment and removal of judges from the Judiciary, from employees and administrative officials, and from members of the army and navy. He exercised the supreme leadership of said military institutes.

IV. LIBERAL PERSISTENCE AND THE CONSTITUTION OF 1867

The administrative reorganization of the country and after the events that drove the dictatorship of Colonel Mariano Ignacio Prado with the consequent war with Spain and the Combat of May 2, 1866, motivated the need to call elections for president and vice president of the Republic, as well as as to the Constituent Congress, unicameral. From that moment, the election of the head of the Executive produced frictions between the Executive and Congress, because Congress did not want to relinquish its audit powers even though it was a constituent, as had already happened with the National Convention of 1856.

The liberals under the initiative of Fernando Casós and del Real had opted for a religious opening, a subject that caused mixed feelings on the rostrum and outside the congress, where a group of sympathizers of the church stoned the anticlerical deputies. Casós accused the government minister José María Gálvez as coverting these attacks, which led to the formulation of the vote of no confidence against said official and therefore against the entire ministerial team, given the nature of being trusted positions. Situation that, for the first time, motivated the resignation in full of the cabinet Tiberiopolis in reference to its holder Pedro José Tordoya, Bishop In Partibus Infidelium (in land of infidels) of

Tiberiópolis, president of the Council of Ministers and Minister of Justice and Worship.

The president, who had previously received a congressional delegation, which expressed the guarantees for the development of the Executive's activities; He refused to accept the resignations of the ministers, who chose to depart. The demolition of the Tiberiopolis cabinet showed the strength of the parliamentary system, provisionally leading to the formation of a cabinet constituted by senior officers and general directors of the ministries until the appointment of their holders, by appointment of confidence of the President of the Republic.

Based on the text of 56, the new Constitution maintained the unicameral conformation. The sessions of the Congress would be held annually with a time of 90 calendar and peremptory days. As for the age to be a representative, it was established that it would be the same as the citizen's, that is, 21 years. For the approval of the norms, the Legislative declared that the bills would be put to the vote after three days of being presented, in that opportunity the procedure to second discussion was dispensed. This entity recovered its interference in the promotions resuming the liberal preach exposed in 1856. Regarding the Executive, the presidential election would be by direct and universal suffrage and failing by the congressional body, extending the mandate to five years. The acts of the agent were valid if they were accompanied by the respective minister, unless the latter had been censured by the Congress. The immediate reelection was maintained.

In the event of a vacancy in the position, the functions were referred to the president of the Council of Ministers. The Legislative supervised the political responsibility of the members of the Executive, as well as that of the magistrates, pronouncing in the first legislature of each constitutional period on the acts of the agent.

The position of Public Prosecutor was replaced by that of Administrative General Prosecutor as consultant to the regime and defender of the interests of the State, whose functions are more similar to those of the current Comptroller General of the Republic. The juntas reappeared, but without the power to claim against the officials appointed by the Ministry of Government, subtracting the degree of interference from the Charter of 1856. The sparse treatment of the municipalities that derived their regulation to the corresponding law was maintained.

The novelty occurred in the Judiciary where an innovative system was proposed: The supreme members were appointed by Congress on the basis of the lists suggested by the same court. The superior vowels were also appointed by the Legislative at the suggestion of the supreme one. The appointments of the judges of right came from the Supreme Court, at the proposal of the Superior and the justices of peace were designated by the Supreme Court, at the proposal of the judges of law. This hierarchy was increased with the establishment of courts for contentious-administrative cases. Despite this design, the regime wanted to put pressure on the judiciary. In 1867 the government demanded fidelity to the judges through an oath to the regime to which the magistrates opposed, who confirmed them when assuming the position.

Although property jobs were abolished, it was declared that only for vacancies or retirement could new places be opened. The direct tax was regulated, making it valid for one year. The commitments generated by the government stemming from the coup d'état were recognized only with the approval of Congress. In the same way, the nullity of the administrative acts produced by those who assumed public functions without the requirements of law was declared. The issue of antimilitarism resumed the liberal preaching, again expressing that military obedience was subordinated to the Constitution and the laws. As for the individual, the granting of nationality was proposed in a flexible way for foreign residents since independence and who had been present in the Combats of Abtao and Callao. Exile and confinement were prohibited, except for declaration of judicial sentence.

On the other hand, human life regained its inviolability by abolishing the death penalty. From August 29, 1867 came into force the new Charter that was not sworn in Arequipa, where the opposition movement burned it publicly and ordered General Pedro Diez Canseco lead the revolt against the regime. The clashes between José Saavedra, Minister of Government and Congressman Mariano Herencia Zevallos, considering that the congress represented an obstacle to the country's march, created a tense situation where Herencia requested that the Legislative Assembly be permanent, a proposal that was seconded, and on the contrary they fell apart until their president Francisco García Calderón closed down in Congress on November 15, 1867.

Given the climate generated by the regime, revolts were fomented, highlighting in the north those coordinated by Colonel José Balta and in the south by Pedro Diez Canseco. Prado could not contain this opposition and preferred to resign on January 5, 1868. Diez Canseco declared the letter of 1867 insubstantial, enforcing the previous one, calling for elections for members of the Executive and representatives to Congress. He highlighted the figure of the hero of Chiclayo, Colonel José Balta, whose speech in favor of recovering the exercise of popular sovereignty and republican purity was successful and well received by the civic clubs (predecessors of the political parties) that supported him.

Elected president of the Republic by the electoral colleges and proclaimed by the Congress, Balta inaugurated his mandate accompanied by Mariano Herencia Zevallos and Francisco Diez Canseco, as first and second vice-president. The handling of the financial crisis in Peru had created friction between the political powers and led to the alternative of granting extraordinary powers to the Executive on the part of Congress. Nicolás de Piérola y Villena, Minister of the Treasury, had gone to the Chamber of Deputies to propose a strategy to improve the national treasury and reduce the deficit, which required the withdrawal of all restrictions on the government. Piérola was inclined to subscribe to the Dreyfus house and brothers, which became the only company that would negotiate the fertilizer once the contracts with national consignees were concluded. In addition, Dreyfus offered to give money to the State to pay the external debt.

Peruvian capitalists aware, asked the government in the next economic management to be granted the benefit of being admitted for their legitimate interest, some of which chose to organize through the party Electoral Independence Society (future Civil Party) to defend their right, declaring Pierola as his enemy.

V. THE FIRST POLITICAL PARTY: THE ELECTORAL INDEPENDENCE SOCIETY

On April 24, 1871, the Electoral Independence Society was born, under the bastions of freedom and autonomy. This new political force began the formation of political parties, harboring the concerns of people from different backgrounds for a better quality of citizenship. Taking as a basis the right of association, Manuel Pardo demonstrated the advantages of the concurrence of wills for a common purpose, where the opinion of the people was important. The nineteenth century illustrates a long road for the arrival of civilians to the office of President of the Republic. The elections before Congress had shown sympathy for the military, the winner of the battles for independence that put order against the deteriorated principle of authority.

From the first moments, civilians identified themselves with ideological tendencies or with the leadership of a character, acting for immediate political purposes. The dilemma between the right to freedom of the individual and the strong government occupied the spaces for discussion, distinguishing the liberals from the conservatives who adopted different positions depending on the regime: monarchists during the administration of San Martin, lifelong or Persian during the dictatorship of Bolivar, Gamarristas between 1829 and 1833, Bermudistas in 1834, confederates between 1835 and 1839, restorers with the return of Gamarra, Vivanquistas or regenerators between 1841 and 1843. The anarchy aroused with the disappearance of Gamarra and the transfer of governmental functions for 4 years, served as an experience for the formation of Club Progreso or Frac, which publicized its ideas in the public opinion through its own journalistic organ and a platform headed by Domingo Elías with the support of Pedro Gálvez and José Sevilla. "The man of the people," as Elias was known to have taken charge of the leadership in the political upheavals, wanted to conquer social groups to face Rufino Echenique in the 1851 elections, whose followers were grouped in the Conservative Society of Constitution and Peace.

Episode that was the preamble of a more integrated version that counted decades later with external elements, as in other areas of South America, and that motivated the arrival of civility to power. The political experience until that moment had shown the inability to plan a stable political project, responsibility both military and of civilians and that prevented to improve the conditions of the country. In the mid-nineteenth century, the political class was aware of this situation and the need to renew the state structure through institutionalized legality and expressed Manual Pardo and Lavalle in his thought: "Sacrifice today to the future." He postulated the reorientation of the governmental role in the economy of the country, with the reduction of expenses and administrative personnel in the State, and at the same time raised a new system of contributions that created its own enemies.

For Pardo, this implied the renegotiation of contracts with national consignees, where it was necessary to reconsider the rights of the State with the best negotiating capacity for its own benefit. However, it was not possible to rescind the harmful contracts to the treasury due to the use of money, by the government, which financed the national budget. The critical situation of the finances had motivated to rethink the establishment of the contributions so as not to depend:

... on a product that is increased with own resources that cover their inferior needs ... ", wrote Manuel Pardo to Mariano Ignacio Prado, December 30, 1865. (El Peruano, 1865).

As minister of Colonel Mariano Ignacio Prado (of the cabinet of the Victory and soon denominated of the Talents by Jorge Basadre) he proposed progressive and proportional instrument in function to the cost of life of each locality of the country. Mechanism that was not sufficiently widespread and, on the other hand, the authorities that carried out its implementation generated conflicts that ended up weakening the approach of the State in its localities. As happened in Huancané, Puno, where criticism emerged under the leadership of Juan Bustamante against the different taxes paid mostly by the Indians: for the financing of the campaign against Spain, for the construction of the cathedral of Puno and the personal contribution. He succeeded in having his manifesto published in El Comercio, so that the congressmen in 1867 could only abolish this contribution. However, there were authorities in the south who continued to charge it, accentuating with it the protests that had a fatal outcome.

Another issue contemplated by the Electoral Independence Society - later the Civil Party - was related to militarism. During the regime of Castilla, the economic stability achieved led to the Congress with the law of February 3, 1848, the Treasury was required to keep the military emerged in each government and revolution, even if they were undefined, that is, without effective placement. Hence, Pardo posed the reduction in the number of personnel that were not career, generating criticism of an army sector that did not surrender to the submission of civility, which embodied the national will.
Previous elections had shown irregularities and violence at the polling stations, a situation that benefited the government itself, which had the means in its favor, to which the indifference of the voters contributed. Pardo proposed the defense of the suffrage by establishing an organization of the electoral system. In May of 1872, the polling stations elected to the president of the Republic a third of the senators and the deputies, all of them of the rows of the party Independence Electoral Society. After the assassination of President Balta and the rebellious brothers Gutiérrez, tranquility returned. The votes in absolute majority granted to Manuel Pardo the first magistrature, being proclaimed by the Congress. The positions of First and Second Vice-President of the Republic, decided by vote in the Legislative, favored Manuel Costas and Francisco Garmendia, respectively.

The civilistes, although betting to create an efficient bureaucracy, knew that they had to do it progressively, due to the lack of resources. Decentralization was considered in the budget, making the distinction between revenues and public expenditures, by classifying them in general (state) and departmental, which demonstrated the existence of needs of local or regional nature, whose solution could be derived to the departments and municipalities with the transfer of resources. In this same section, the government opted for the desacralization of state functions that had remained in the parishes. The law of 1873 optionally established the registration of population data such as births, marriages and deaths in the municipalities, alternating with that of the parish books.

Culturally, Pardo's Plan del Perú was progressively recreating the analysis of the Andean reality that it saw parallel to the capitalist until it later integrated it as its complement given that the reality of the Andes included its own system of economic rationality (Mc Evoy, 1994, pp. 239-249). Aspect that, although it was not valued by the Peruvian State yet, but it was by the landowners, who adopted a leading role as notable in the area.

VI. THE WAR WITH CHILE AND THE CONSTITUTIONAL BREAKDOWN: THE PROVISIONAL STATUTE OF 1879 AND THE TREATY OF ANCON

The 1878 treasury crisis and the declaration of war by Chile to Peru, motivated a rethinking of the resources to face this adversity. With the authorization of the Council of Ministers and Congress, through the legislative resolution of May 9, 1879, President Mariano Ignacio Pardo traveled to Europe and the United States to personally acquire weapons and vessels, leaving the command to Vice President Luis La Puerta de Mendoza. Before the vacuum, Nicolás de Piérola supported by a sector of the army gave the coup that allowed him to declare himself Dictator of Peru, on December 23. Days later he named his secretaries of state: Pedro José Calderón (Foreign Affairs and Worship), Federico Panizo (Justice and instruction), Mariano Echegaray (Development), Miguel Iglesias (War), Manuel Villar (Navy) and Manuel A. Barinaga (Treasure).

Subsequently issued with them, the Provisional Statute of 1879, whose articles guaranteed rights and freedoms within the confessional framework but also aggravated the penalties criminalizing behavior in case of insubordination, cowardice, fraud of public property, premeditated and treacherous homicide, as well as other analogous facts that would be judged by military court. He abolished the departmental councils of 1873.

This episode was not aliening to impose a cultural policy in favor of the regime. Piérola in his eagerness that the dictatorship had the support of the community and especially the large inarticulate sector as the rural declared Protector of the Indian Race, which although in the recital notes that motivated the injustices committed and their prompt replacement, the fact is that the war demanded the incorporation of more men to form the battalions that would have their outcome in the famous battles of San Juan and Miraflores, where the soldiers spoke Quechua and Aymara and the officers, Castilian. The paternalistic role of the administration can be contemplated in the norm, in substitution of the judicial Power, directed to the solution of land disputes between the peasants and the landowners:

"Art 2.- The individuals and corporations belonging to this race have the right to appeal directly to me, in word or in writing, against any abuse, injustice or denial of this that they suffered from any authority whatever their name and hierarchy, being excempted from the common laws in this regard. " (Decree of May 22, 1880)

The loss of military forces caused that the Chilean offensive arrived at the capital, motivated the displacement of the government to the mountain range. Meanwhile, General Manuel Baquedano Gonzales, head of the occupation army, who preferred to flee before surrendering the capital unconditionally. Hubert Wieland portrays the circumstances that in this crisis accompanied the power vacuum that culminated in the interview with Rufino Torrico, Mayor Lima, who made available to Baquedano the City of Kings without conditions. Fact that counted on the presence of foreign diplomats to avoid the excesses of the victory of the Chileans:

"In the first place, because of the considerable number of resident foreigners that it housed; second, by the determination of the diplomatic corps accredited in Peru, in particular by the ministers of Great Britain and France, and by the leaders of the squads of both powers and of the Italian, to defend the lives and interests of their nationals ; and, finally, due to the fact that the destruction of the three Peruvian towns mentioned had already taken place, which was a clear omen of what could be the destiny of Lima "(Wieland, 2017).

In Ayacucho, Piérola convened the National Assembly, which installed on July 28 and submitted its resignation. Meanwhile, the Board of Notables in the City of Kings appointed Francisco García Calderón Landa, dean of the Lima Bar Association, as president of Peru on March 12, 1881, who enjoyed the recognition of the Chilean authorities at the beginning. He abolished the Statute of Pierola and restored the validity of the Constitution of 1860.

García Calderón convened extraordinary sessions of the Congress with members who had remained until last November, meeting in the Beach Resort

of Chorillos on May 15. The collegiate counted with 32 representations, some of which were temporary with the citizens residing in Lima until their replacement with the holders. The primary interest of the collegiate was directed to the discussion of the terms of peace in the negotiations with Chile, prevailing the prohibition of territorial cession and that did not have unanimous agreement and precipitated the conclusion of the sessions on August 22, 1881.
Attitude that did not please the occupation army or its government that ordered an end to the regime of President García Calderón who had already expressed his refusal to sign the peace agreement with the corresponding delivery of Tarapacá to the southern country. Both he and his Minister Manuel María Gálvez, Minister of Foreign Affairs, were arrested and banished to Valparaíso. Weeks later, General Miguel Iglesias, former Minister of the Dictatorship of 1879, with his proclamation of Montan (name of his hacienda) raised the urgency of achieving peace with Chile, giving up the coastal province of Tarapacá. At the same time, Iglesias convened an assembly in Cajamarca with representatives from the northern part of the country: Cajamarca, Piura, Lambayeque, La Libertad, Ancash, Amazonas and Loreto, which finally began its sessions on December 30, 1882.

The absence of García Calderón created the conditions for the establishment of a new regime under the President Regenerator of the Republic and a general minister who was his brother Colonel Lorenzo Iglesias. In Arequipa, in parallel Admiral Lizardo Montero with a parallel representation in two chambers began his duties, on April 22, 1883. He maintained García Calderón as president of the Republic, detained in Valparaíso, naming Montero and Andrés Avelino Cáceres as first and second vice-president, respectively. The Legislative completed the list of representatives with local citizens. Given the attitude of the collegiate in not giving up any territory, the Chilean regime did not recognize it and maintained its operation until June 20 of the same year.

During this time, Admiral Montero ruled that, since the Supreme Court in Lima occupied by the Chilean army had been suspended and to avoid prejudice due to the paralysis of the trials, that this collegiate with its members and administrative staff resumed work in Arequipa (Decree November 25, 1882). The southern assembly was not recognized by Chile and continued its operation until October 22 when the Chilean army occupied Ayacucho. Meanwhile, in Cajamarca the Legislative Power with Chilean sympathy opted to end the warlike climate which materialized in the signing of the Treaty of Peace and Friendship between the republics of Peru and Chile or Treaty of Ancon, on October 20, 1883. Under the supervision of the army of occupation four days later the government of Lima convened a third constituent assembly, whose elections took place in Lima directly. Once installed, on March 1 of the following year Miguel Iglesias y Pino was appointed Provisional President of the Republic, beginning the second militarism.

VII. THE RESTORATION OF CONSTITUTIONALISM AND THE SECOND MILITARISM

The Congress approved the Treaty of Ancon in secret session; nevertheless, he pointed out that, having been produced, the necessary conditions and political stability did not exist due to the Chilean occupation that lasted for six more months, which prevented compliance. It declared in force the 1860 constitution but introducing variations: No more contributions could be established except in terms of the possibilities of its taxpayer holder and for the public good. The Executive decided on the income and expenditures of the Nation, appointment of magistrates, renewal of authorities; also had the discretion to generate new resources. Circumstance that shows us the leadership of this power of the State that by regulation determined the establishment of Departmental Fiscal Boards chaired by the Prefect and composed of delegates from the provinces.

Although the intention was to collect and monitor the use of public resources, the State preferred to maintain the centralist profile, the Juntas were maintained, but lacked resources, since there were provinces that had suffered the inclemencies of war, including Ayacucho, Junín and Huancavelica. Months later in the month of November, there was an offensive that ended with clashes in the capital and ended up surrounding the regime. Since then, a whole process of agreements with the intervention of the diplomatic corps was initiated so that Iglesias and Cáceres renounced the power they exercised. Commissioners were appointed by the two parties to the conflict, and the Council of Ministers was designated as the transitory organ, which called for elections after Iglesias resigned on December 3, 1885.

In the judicial, President Iglesias created a commission investigating and rating to take accounts to any state entity on funds managed, received or spent during the war in and outside the republic. (Decree of November 9, 1883). The constitution of 1860 was declared in force; but with modifications among which it was indicated: The Executive decided on the income and expenses of the Nation, appointment of magistrates, renewal of authorities; he also had the authorization to generate new resources and make the changes at his discretion. The administration could not escape the criticism arising from the scope of the Treaty of Ancon, generating even a fierce opposition from the army itself led by Colonel Andrés Avelino Cáceres Dorregaray, head of the resistance during the occupation, which triggered the civil war. Situation that ended the regime on December 3, 1885 and giving way to the convening of general elections.

The Constitutional Party composed of some members of the Civil Party, presented Cáceres as its candidate. Only the Democratic Party with Nicolás de Piérola was the alternative. The Civilistas who led the Congress in the person of Francisco Rosas leaned towards the Hero of Breña.

In spite of the great expectation of management for the fame of the president and the optimism of the president of the Congress, on August 3 the questioning of the Minister of Finance Luis N. Bryce was raised at the initiative of the Finance Commissions and Infractions due to the liquidation of the pending debts with the Peruvian Guano as well as the Dreyfus House and for the convenience of initiating a process abroad against these two companies. The minister had presented a budget that was objected by these commissions, which in turn decided to redo it, not granting Bryce the right to propose another alternative. This attitude of the Deputies against the regime was evidenced months later with the management of Minister Manuel Irigoyen. The degree of prostration of the Treasury, due to the state deficit and the difficulties of circulation between fiscal notes due to the lack of support, created tense situations for the censorship of the cabinet to be requested.

The Chamber of Deputies agreed to the constitutional accusation in accordance with article 59 of the 1860 constitution and the law of September 28, 1868 against Manuel Irigoyen and Pedro Alejandrino del Solar, which was passed on to the Senate, which ultimately did not subscribe. The new president of the Council of Ministers Carlos M. Elías told Congress that, due to the nature of the Grace contract signed between José Araníbar, fiscal agent in Europe and the representative of the Peruvian bondholders, its terms could motivate divergence with Chile in his capacity as signatory to the Treaty of Ancon, even claiming that he could not submit it to the Legislative discussion.

Affirmation that caused a stir because it was questioned whether the benefit should be for the country or for Chile, causing the beginning of the process of censorship against the cabinet. Situation that did not prosper because its members resigned before the approval of such measure and that generated, similar to the experience of 1867, the cabinet of the directors. On November 8, 1887, a new Council of Ministers was formed, presided over by the second vice president of the Republic Aurelio Denegri and composed mostly of members of Congress. Three days later, the extraordinary legislature was closed with the approval of the recognition of the service of the internal debt that had been regulated by rules from 1873 and that had generated interest. However, the way in which the conversion of the different currencies (fiscal and Inca notes) which became monies ended up damaging the certificate holders, who contemplated the depreciation of their debts.

The minority had chosen to delay the discussion of the Grace Contract as the best weapon to manifest their opposition, reaching unsuspected limits with Quimper's long speeches. After the closing of the sessions and before the existence of impasses among the members of the Legislative, the majority established new rules for the renewal of the opposition minority which was considered to:

"... disable the procedures of the majority or avoids its decisions "(Basadre, 2000, volume 8, p. 2044).

On May 20, the Third Extraordinary Congress took office, which considered the matter of the Grace Contract, concluding it in all its terms. The atmosphere was different from the previous Congresses, limited to proposing amendments in the document to be negotiated, which were accepted by the representative of the bondholders. This law that authorized the contract included another rule with the intervention of Chile, given that the nature of the renegotiation included aspects of the Ancon Treaty, which were linked to the delivery of guano to the southern country.

The elections of 1890, unlike previous, Civilism presented its own candidates: Francisco García Calderón Landa and Francisco Rosas Balcázar that brought together both landowners, miners, soldiers, lawyers and priests. For his part, Cáceres presented Remigio Morales Bermúdez as his successor, with the support of Mariano N. Valcárcel, president of the Chamber of Deputies. There was the renewal of the third in deputies with the majority of the Constitutional Party while in senators were the Civilistas. This did not stop confrontations between the government and society, such as the attempted assault on the Santa Catalina barracks that killed 20 people, despite their surrender.

With the purpose of the renovation of the Chambers in 1892, the political forces were measured between the Constitutionalists (some Civilists) and the genuine Constitutionalists (supporters of Cáceres). Mariano Nicolás Valcárcel as president of the Chamber of Deputies and Francisco Rosas, in the senators came to the conviction that it was necessary to create a front against the interference of militarism based on Civilists and some Constitutionalists, which gave rise to the Civic Union as an alternative to the government party.
At the cultural level, there was legal recognition of the ownership of land by indigenous people - as a precursor to the constitutional incorporation of the communities - in the district of Cabana, province of Lucanas (October 30, 1893). The Prefects of the Departmental Boards were excluded, provided that they

were left in charge of the elected authorities (October 24, 1893). With the elections of 1894 coming, the political forces were divided between the Civic Union, the Constitutional Party or Cacerista and the Democrat or Pierolista.

In the face of the sudden death of President Remigio Morales Bermúdez, the second vice-president, Colonel Justiniano Borgoño, called not only the third to be renewed, but also the entire chamber. In the electoral process, the same policy of replacing the municipalities by the Board of Notables was maintained, a fact that generated abstentions except those of the official party.

The election of Andrés A. Cáceres, as the new president, fruit of the pressure of his party, led to a tense relationship with groups in the community, and the government ordered the suspension of individual guarantees. Criticism came from different social circles and opposition parties, who decided to make the first national agreement that would end the presence of military in power.

In different parts of the country, the protests did not wait: Oswaldo Seminario, Augusto Durand, Santiago Oré, Nicolás de Piérola and Amador del Solar, represented the opposition of urban and rural areas in Piura, Huánuco, Ica, Chincha and Arequipa, respectively. The government imposed more taxes so that the forces of the order could fight them, even the budgetary items of the payment of the external debt were excluded as the resources of financing of the departments.

The pressure of the population unleashed a confrontation with the entrance to Lima of a contingent on horseback to Lima through the Cocharcas gate, on March 17, 1895. The force led by Nicolás de Piérola and the other leaders fought against the forces of the order, causing thousands of deaths and injuries, on both sides. Situation that forced to an armistice and to the conformation of a meeting of Government in charge of Manuel Candamo, that counted on the intervention of diplomats, to maintain the appeasement. Cáceres opted to resign and the board called for elections on April 14, whose result favored Nicolás de Piérola with the support of the Civilistas, ending the second militarism.

CHAPTER FOUR

The return of civilians and the third militarism

I. THE CONSTITUTIONALISM AD-PORTAS OF THE XX CENTURY: THE RETURN OF PIÉROLA

The decree of April 14 called for general elections in accordance with the law of 1861. The Congress in qualifying the minutes determined the victory of Nicolás de Piérola and Villena as president of the Republic accompanied by Guillermo Billinghurst and Augusto Seminario as first and Second Vice President of the Republic. The new members of the Legislative, in the month of September, proposed motions to remove from the roster generals Caceres, Mas and Borgoño and declare without effect the rules produced by this power the previous year that sought to apply criminal liability against opponents of the regime.

However, the Senate through the Committees of Constitution, Legislation and Infractions was pronounced against the removal of the ladder arguing that such sanction was not attribution of the Congress, in any case, elaborated the text of the law of December 20, 1895 which repealed the one which proclaimed Andrés Avelino Cáceres as President of the Republic. The processing of the accusations was referred to the Judicial Power and the Executive limited itself to declaring the administrative resolutions of the previous regimes null and void and to grant the political amnesty until the formation of the Governing Board under Senator Manuel Candamo. Piérola when assuming the command initiated a whole period of civil institutionality. For him, Congress should keep:

"... its separation in two Chambers, of different origins in its composition, with peculiar attributions to each one and relation with the functions that they must carry in the federative form" (Patrtido Demócrata, 1912, p.30)

The loss of the war and the disappearance of the second militarism gave the propitious moment to propose a new conception of the State: bureaucrat, stable and participatory of suffrage (through political parties). Bureaucrat, through the use of the resources of the country in a climate of stability, fighting the natural and acquired difficulties that would allow achieving well-being.

The public employment would be given according to the aptitude, not creating dependency of the beneficiary with respect to who granted it, since this one represented the Nation in that moment. Its number would be subject to a fiscal administration and supervision, which would eventually be entrusted to the future Ministry of Development (law of January 22, 1896), depending on the transfer of income to the Departmental Boards (law of October 21, 1897).

The army, an important instrument of the State, was the institution to which the prestige and morality had to be returned, for which a new regulation was given regarding the promotions under military norms (law of September 27, 1898), which included the universal and compulsory military service. To this we must add the interest of civility in providing a professional organization, but above all apolitical, according to the changes in neighboring countries, which would be achieved with the invitation of the French military mission to take charge of the Military Academy of Chorrillos. Finally, the State should be participatory, through the collaboration of political forces, whose organization and program provided security to the democratic system.

For its part, the judicial body should be more technical and apolitical, for which it should be provided with stability in the post, declaring the judges permanent and well paid. While it is true that the Constitution and the law granted independence, in fact a legal will was required to consolidate its impartial functioning. In the Executive, in fact, tried to separate the leadership of the

President of the Republic moving to the President of the Council of Ministers, in this way the first president was excluded from the audit, which would allow him to act more independently. For its part, each minister would enjoy complete autonomy in the management of his portfolio, coordinating with the Treasury to have funds. The commitments acquired by the previous regimes were acknowledged, both abroad and in the country, as a reflection of the trust in the State that had the will to do so, the ability to pay them, with the resources and the direction to guide the credit to a specific need. The economy to be sanitized required a stability whose image would be achieved with the gold standard applied to the Peruvian pound, allocating the silver and copper coins for other transactions, while the notes would be issued by a single entity.

The law of November 20, 1897 proposed the new organization in charge of the National Electoral Board, departmental boards, provincial boards and district delegations. The existence of an electoral registry and of the counting boards facilitated the proclamation of president and vice president of the Republic. The vote was public and direct. During this period, the Habeas Corpus law was also approved (October 21, 1897), culminating the project that came five years ago and that had as its objective to regulate article 18 of the Charter of 1860. The political context between the end of the second militarism and the return of civilians had increased arbitrary arrests and demanded its prompt regulation.

On the other hand, Pierola had expressed to the new legislature, through a message, his criticism of the right to enact laws from ordinary legislatures in extraordinary sessions, referring in a concrete manner to the approval of the Budget of the Republic. As for the balance of power in the elections of 1897, the Civilists ratified their alliance with the Democrats, which was not seconded by some members of the latter party as Augusto Durand, who then created the

Independent Circle, base of the next Liberal Party. To all this it was added that the Chamber of Deputies became a forum adverse to the government, which questioned the validity of the governmental measures and took the defense of the Departmental Boards against the centralization of the government.

In the middle of this restoration of the system, voices of vindication of the indigenous group were raised, above all in a pacification that the country claimed after the War with Chile. Manuel Gonzales Prada, liberal anarchist, presented us, in the Tetaro del Politeama, his famous speech (1888) where he proposed a reconstruction of the State and of society, seeking, in the first place, the validity of the institutions and reassessing the role of the indigenous people. As an integral part of the nation should be provided education, which would lead to the defense of their rights in the best way: If we made a servant of the Indian, what country will defend? As the servant of the Middle Ages, he will only fight for the feudal lord (Gonzales 1888).

Javier Prado Ugarteche, in his famous speech on "The social state of Peru during the Spanish domination (1894)", came to the conclusion that the Indian had become quieter and more servile after the conquest. To remedy the difficulties in its integration, it had to be formed through education with the intention of placing it according to the expectations of the new national industry. It determined the need for repopulation with the presence of European immigrants. Ideas that acted in parallel to the need for the formation of an elite with moral and cultural values. Educated to govern, she would find in the oligarchy her closest reflection. Concern expressed by Francisco García Calderón Rey which would serve as an ideological course for the second civilismo, whose members had already been nourished by Pardo's proposals. The vision of the Indian, in Alejandro Deustua (The National Culture), was circumscribed to the labor aspect since education-according to him-could only be provided to capable people, because the Indian could not help but be a machine.

II. THE BIPARTIDISM: THE DEMOCRAT PARTY AND THE RETURN OF THE CIVIL PARTY

On July 28, 1899, Eduardo Lopez de Romaña became the next president of the Republic and with him the Civilist-Democratic alliance was preserved, but with certain difficulties, there was a schism within the Pierolistas, who considered that it was necessary to recover autonomy in the political line. Despite the existence of civilians in both organs of power and with some opposition, there was a zeal for the preservation of attributions of both political powers. The Executive maintained the policy of not giving due process to those laws approved in extraordinary sessions and that did not respond to the matters of its convocation. Circumstances that created hostilities between political powers and the subsequent resignation of the cabinet of Manuel María Gálvez Egúsquiza, that did not stop the appetite or Pierolistas Democrats with a majority in the Lower House while Civilistas retained the leadership in the Senate). Attitude that sharpened the censorship, producing the resignation of twelve ministers, considering that there were six per cabinet.

The censorship of Manuel Domingo Almenara Butler, president of the Council of Ministers, on August 13, 1901 was due to the appointment of the Board of Notables for the municipal elections instead of calling elections. Although he had the support of the Chamber of Senators he did not get rid of the Deputies. The second censored cabinet was headed by Alejandro Deustua Escarza, president of the Council of Ministers and head of the government ministry. In those years the conversations with the government of Ecuador had advanced to define the border delimitations, which were qualified as harmful to the country, being harmful to the country.

It was the turn of Cesáreo Chacaltana's cabinet to confront the claims of the Chucuito Indians regarding the mistreatment of those who were victims, a fact that caused the interpellation of the Government Minister Leónidas Cárdenas. This episode that will involve several governments and congresses allowing us to contemplate the little presence of the State in areas that recurrently convulsed. It was so that the following year Alejandrino Maguiña was commissioned by President Candamo to study the reason for these complaints in Juli, Puno, generated by the abuses of the landowners, as well as the partialization of the own mayors and judges of first instance, who promoted or seconded forced services, the establishment of taxes on wool producers and the arbitrary collection of property taxes.

Years later, the sub-prefect of Chucuito, sergeant major Teodomiro Gutiérrez Cuevas intervened in favor of the Indians, which earned him being slandered and even denounced by the deputies and senators of Puno, demanding the vacancy of the office. Later, losing government support and being fought by the farmers of Puno, he retired to Bolivia and reappeared as an indigenous leader called Rumi Maqui (Stone Hand). His insurrection was defeated by the forces of order and his leader captured and tried for treason. After the sentence will disappear without leaving traces. In spite of everything, the Maguiña report revealed the approach of the government and then of the Legislative one in the diagnosis of the national problems, whose corrective measures ended up being ineffective due to the pressure of the landowners themselves due to the little presence of the State.

Meanwhile, before the bipartisanship in power, emerged the Liberal Party, as a new political force, in charge of Augusto Durand made the members of the Legislative, especially the Democrats, saw in them the recovery of the spirit of oversight - in more strict- of the governmental acts that until that moment had been engrossed or diluted between Democrats and Civilists. The former Democrats insisted that, prior to the occupation of a new government office, political responsibility should be set aside.

In addition, the Liberals postulated the declaration of unconstitutionality of the laws by the Supreme Court, the defense of indigenous communities, the separation of the Church-State bond with the consequent full exercise of other religions; the defense of the right of assembly, decentralization, etc. However, its political presence remained in second place due to the prominence that Pierola still had from the opposition. In the economic sphere, the regime retained the Democratic plan regarding the issuance of the Peruvian Pound of Gold and silver coins of 9 tenths and those of copper for the cents; providing confidence to the market. The law of November 22, 1901, tried to avoid distortions in the promotion of military force, limiting them to competitions under criteria of seniority and aptitude. The then Indian ordinances were replaced by the first Code of Military Justice of December 20, 1899.

The bipartisanship was not only affected by the emersion of the other political forces but by the cracking of the Civil party itself. With the presence of Manuel Candamo had achieved the desired refoundation, but his sudden death while serving as president of Peru, opened a space between the members of the old and new guard of the group, the latter led by José Pardo y Barreda and integrated by Augusto B. Leguía. Both future presidents in the successive electoral processes. However, Leguía would distance himself from the Civilistas at the moment of starting his administration. Tense situation that hosted a recomposition in the Congress, varying the number of seats of the official party with members of Leguiismo in the renewal by thirds. The experience of the then president paved the way for voters in the 1912 campaign to prefer Guillermo Billinghust, Angulo, who replaced Piérola, now deceased, in the leadership of the Democrats. Faithful to its denomination, its electoral campaign was characterized by reivindicativas measures for the workers and for that reason it was known him like Big Bread in front of its contender Antero Aspìllaga Barrera, civilista leader.

The attitude of the new president, for his proximity to the labor sectors deployed measures that sought to democratize the mechanisms of the political system, innovated the rules to expand the electoral base, under the argument that who pays taxes, votes. Later, Congress amended the plan indicating that only large taxpayers had the right to suffrage. Gradually, the Executive-Legislative relationship deteriorated, in the most critical moments the postponement of the approval of the general budget of the corresponding republic of 1912 until the following year made the government by decree of December 29 of that year, become charge of finance, without congressional support. Situation that would be collected decades later as constitutional attribution of the Executive. Billinghurst was inclined for the total renewal of the congress, prior dissolution. Measure that would be accompanied by reforms that involved.

The decrease in the number of representatives -especially those that appeared as a result of the more political than technical creation of new provinces-; the extension of the legislature when the national budget did not get approved, dedicating itself exclusively to it. In addition, the prohibition of the exercise of any administrative function be public or private while serving as a congressman. The disappearance of the figure of the vice presidents of the Republic, because in case of vacancy, the president of the Senate assumed the position temporarily. The right of the government to regulate the salaries of public officials. The establishment of the national referendum or referendum as an alternative to the decisions of the Congress, if both showed the popular will. The set of these proposals coincided with those of Mariano H. Cornejo and Javier Prado, which allowed some of them to be studied and approved by the Legislative. Billinghust, although it was rooted among the majority sectors, especially workers and artisans, did not decide to arm the population to exert pressure and subdue the congress. The first days of the following month there were arrests, requests for political asylum and closure of the media.

The rebels of the garrison of Lima marched to Palace and achieved the resignation of the President of the Republic, who agreed to such a claim (El Comercio, February 4, 1914). In its replacement a Board of Notables was established, whose members mostly came from the Congress. On May 15 of that year, a motion proposed Colonel Oscar R. Benavides as Provisional President of the Republic, which was formalized by legislative resolution No. 1958, the Board of Notables disappearing and the congressional body declaring itself in recess until its installation on the eve of the Independence Day. In the elections of May 16, 1915, the Civilists, prior National Convention, reached a consensus among the different political shops, defeating José Pardo and Barreda as president of the Republic, accompanied by Ricardo Bentín and Melitón Carbajal as first and second vice-president, respectively. At the political level in 1919, there was the intention of holding another convention or modality that would bring the parties together like what happened with José Pardo; but no agreement was reached because each of them already had its own candidate.

Due to its distance from the country, the figure of Leguía had been strengthened by presenting itself as an alternative to the other political stores, as was perceived in the election results in Lima and Callao. Despite being favorite in the minutes and as the process concluded, there were observations in them. Circumstance that warned that the last decision in the presidential election would have the Parliament with a civilian majority betting on its contender Antero Aspillaga, former adversary of Billinghurst.

With the coup led by Leguía, the bipartisanship project, created since 1895, came to an end and was replaced by a reformist regime that would affect the structure of the State like the democracy of that time.

III. LA PATRIA NUEVA AND THE STATE REFORMS

The uprising of July 4, 1919 meant in political terms the end of the Aristocratic Republic and the Civil Party in the regime due to the erosion of the exercise of power and lack of renewal mechanisms. But this date also marked the beginning of the New Homeland, in defense of national interests, the establishment of legislation that ensures public order that does not ignore the exercise of rights, the:

"... cultural and material development for social assistance and for the protection of the indigenous race, for the granting of laws for the improvement and advancement of the working classes and for guaranteeing harmony between capital and work ..." (Guerra Martiniére, 1988, Volume IX, p.192).

Approaches that were the programmatic bases of the Democratic Reformist Party or Leguïsta, endorsement of the governmental and legislative acts. The idea of the establishment of this new order was not conciliatory because the Justicialist ministers, unlike their previous counterparts, did not seek rapprochement with the other political forces, which explains the lack of amnesty laws. It was the first time that four congresses were alternated simultaneously, (the national, one of the north, center and south of the country) reflecting the decentralization from the congress organ as opposed to the other governmental alternatives.

The Congress to be formed as a National Assembly would have as its mission the reform of the Constitution. Through the plebiscite, a mechanism previously proposed by Billinghurst, the following aspects were submitted to the decision of the electorate: The total renewal of the Legislative that would coincide with that of the Executive's mandate, every five years. The Congress would be composed of 35 senators and 110 deputies, elected by direct popular vote and will work from 90 to 120 days a year. Individual guarantees could not be suspended by any law or authority. The next Congress would be installed on September 15 presided over by the president of the Senate and will operate for 30 days as a National Assembly to promulgate constitutional reforms.

From these proposals we distinguish approaches aimed at establishing guarantees in favor of the individual as well as innovations in the existing state organization. To this was incorporated the operation of the State Council and the parallel march of three Regional Congresses, with the following jurisdictions: North: The departments of Piura, Lambayeque, La Libertad, Ancash, Cajamarca, Loreto and Amazonas, as well as the province of Tumbes. Center: The departments of Lima, Junín, Huánuco, Ica, Huancavelica,

Ayacucho, and the Constitutional Province of Callao. South: The departments of Arequipa, Tacna, Cusco, Apurímac, Puno, Madre de Dios, and the province of Moquegua. Congresses that in practice were subordinated to the Central Power, seeing themselves reduced to act as initiative entities, because their rules could be vetoed by the Legislative or the Government.

The National Assembly installed on September 24, 1919 embodied the renewal of the Legislative, whose doctrinal leadership was shared between Mariano H. Cornejo and Javier Prado Ugarteche. In it we also find other forces such as the Democrats with Carlos de Piérola; Leguiístas: Eduardo Basadre and Enrique Oyaguren; Liberals: Lauro Curletti and Eduardo La Natta and Constitutionalists: César Canevaro and Augusto Bedoya. Retroactively, Law 3083 was passed, which granted validity to the devices issued by the regime between July 4 and the proclamation of the Constitutional President of the Republic:

"The National Assembly: Exercising the fullness of the Constituent Power that has conferred the plebiscite ... Has given the following constitutional law:

Art. 1. - Approve all the acts practiced by the Provisional Government to take charge of the Power, to summon the peoples to the national plebiscite and to preserve order.

Art. 2.- All the decrees issued by the Provisional Government have the force of law.

Art. 3.- The Provisional Government will continue to exercise the Executive Power until the day it is proclaimed Constitutional President "(García Belaunde, 2016, p.413).

Then the Legislature made the count for the elections, with Augusto B. Leguía as the president of the Republic, and then César Canevaro and Agustín Torres Gonzáles as first and second vice-presidents, respectively. In addition to this, because the Constituent Assembly was to confer the power to extend the presidential term of four to five years, the same that would end on October 12, 1924. In the following session, the Constitution Committee was formed the draft Constitution based on the result of the plebiscite, which was to be approved by a third of the senators and deputies. Some of these, like Manuel Frisancho, understood that the plebiscitary measures were aimed at reforming the Constitution of 1860, but not replacing it. Of the complementary laws referring to the reforms, only those related to the Council of State and the diplomatic service were issued throughout the Eleventh Year. As for decentralization, the entity par excellence represented in the municipality was absent in the elections, its conformation was subject to the designations made by the Executive.

As for the Executive, it was established that the mandate for president of the Republic lasted five years, not being able to be re-elected except for an immediate period (articles 113 and 119 of the Constitution of 1920). But as Leguia's power deepened, Congress issued Law No. 4687 (September 19, 1923) that reformed the device, stipulating that he could be re-elected for an immediate and one-time period. Years later, the same body gave the law No. 5857 eliminating such restriction, leaving the way clear for reelection without any limitation. The functions of deputy or senator were limited while the ministerial position was exercised. The vote of no confidence, issued by one or both houses, forced this official to resign.

The novelty in this Constitution was the return of the Council of State that served as a hinge between the Congress and the Executive. Its members were appointed by the Council of Ministers and ratified by the Senate. As for the Regional Congresses, the Deputies worked in parallel with their national counterparts, however, their session lasted only thirty days a year. Magistrates were prohibited from playing a political role.

Opinion in clear allusion to the protagonism of Germán Leguía y Martínez, member of the Supreme Court and then Minister of Government, known for denying the writs of Habeas Corpus and who would end up being a victim later of his cousin's own dictatorship. A major point of the Charter of 1920 was that of national, social and individual guarantees that are placed in the worldwide changes with the Constitution of Weimar (Germany) and Queretaro of 1917 (Mexico). The distinction in the Peruvian case varied according to the right invoked: if it was inherent in the person or if it was a function of their duty to society. Within this contribution can be seen the confusion in the writing of the corresponding chapters to include the rights (which constituted the main part) with the guarantees (which were its protective mechanisms).

Constitutionally, it was stipulated that the laws also protected and obliged everyone, establishing special laws only because of the nature of things (Article 17). No one could be arrested without a written warrant from the competent judge except for flagrante delicto. In the face of arbitrary measures, the detained person or any other person could file habeas corpus (article 24). The statements obtained by force, the convictions made by judges of different competence, as well as the execution of laws that did not exist at the time of committing the imputed act, legally invalidated the act (Article 26). Despite stressing these constitutional measures, the government practice came into conflict on different occasions.

Culturally, it should be noted in the Charter of 1920 the recognition of the legal existence of indigenous communities in the constitutional field, thereby resolving the consequences that had led to its abolition since 1825. In the first place, the State provided protection of the indigenous race, deriving from the legal scope the rights that correspond to them, among others, the promotion for their development (articles 57º and 58º). As Basadre points out, the legal system in a dispersed way had already granted such recognition:

"The legislative resolution of October 11, 1893 ... declared that the Indians were legitimate owners of the lands they owned ... the Water Code recognized the existence of the communities, as well as the law of roads of 2 of November 1916 "(Basadre, 2000, Volume 11, p. 2877).

On the other hand, it was declared that the assets of the indigenous communities together with those of the State were imprescriptible, being transferable only by public title (article 41). This protest speech was complemented with the creation of the Section of Indigenous Affairs in the Ministry of Public Works and Development, the creation of the Board of the Indigenous Race, the operation of schools in the countryside, as well as the establishment of the Day of the Indian.

Under the auspices of this proposal of democracy there was also a rapprochement of the government towards the new industrialists and the middle class, which contrasted with the constant arbitrary measures. To the protests generated by the denial of the resources of Habeas Corpus, the Minister of Government Germán Leguía y Martínez responded that these were only granted in cases of abuse of authority or as a guarantee of "honest citizens", and that the acts had developed during the mandate of the provisional government had already had the support of the National Assembly through Law No. 3083.

Criticism from the media and the university faculty led to new repressive measures, including the arrest of Luis Fernán Cisneros, director from the newspaper La Prensa; the deportation of Augusto Durand its owner, and the expropriation of this newspaper. To this were added in the following months, the deportations of: Víctor Andrés Belaúnde (Dean of the Faculty of Arts of the Universidad Mayor de San Marcos), Oscar R. Benavides (former President of the Republic), of the Deputies Pedro Ruiz Bravo (representative of Antabamba), Juan Manuel Torres Balcázar (representative of Lima) and Manuel Prado Ugarteche (representative of Huamachuco); of the university leader Víctor Raúl Haya de la Torre and in 1923 of Germán Leguía y Martínez himself, who, far from the cabinet and as a Deputy from Lima, opposed the re-election of his cousin, receiving as a sanction the same measure that he applied as minister of Government.

The Congress, on the initiative of the representative of Puno José Encinas, created a research commission to analyze the riots in Cusco and Puno, socially sensitive places where the gamonales still kept the practices of forced labor or enganche, to benefit from the free workforce.

El Oncenio, in those places where he could not impose his power, was forced to continue with existing local or regional influences such as those of Luis F. Luna, deputy for Sandia or Enrique Torres Belón, deputy for Lampa, who agreed to your political proposal. Within the new created order we find a series of public works financed with international loans from the United States and authorized by Congress since 1922 through Law No. 4387 (July 14, 1922) for 5 million dollars. Sum that was gradually ascending to that authorized by law No. 5930 (December 18, 1927), worth 100 million dollars known as the "Peruvian National Loan", which was used to refinance the external debt and the execution of the works like the public service in the capital of the country and of other centers in the interior, as well as the projects of colonization. For the latter, Law No. 4113 or road conscription law was enacted, which would provide labor from men between 18 and 60 years old, whether Peruvian or foreign: The government's road policy affected the control they had over the ways.

In addition, the road law forced the mobilization of hacienda workers without considering the calendar of agricultural activities on the coast. Under a purpose of participation, corruption was created because the authorities soon became the exploiters themselves. In addition, the regime did not accept the existence of an idle labor force, a situation contemplated in Law No. 4891, which considered vagrancy as a phenomenon opposed to the wishes of the State, comprising in it all individuals, of legal age, who in conditions to fend for himself, do not work. The interest for the survival of the Leguiista power caused that the military ticket was used for the following process of elections, discarding the registers of contributors. The elections were direct and public, opting to assign to the Congress the function of counting votes for the President of the Republic, proclaiming it later.

It should be noted that, although there was an approach between the Executive and the Legislative that allowed the lack of opposition between the two since 1924, the panorama was exceptionally altered by the issue of the Solomon-Lozano Boundary Treaty, which dealt with border delimitation with Colombia. The clauses had indicated, in favor of Colombia, the Amazonian Trapeze and in counterpart Peru had the Triangle of Sucumbios, which would end up being delivered by our country to Ecuador with the signing of the respective Protocol in 1942. In spite of having signed the Treaty of Limits in 1922, this was not approved until after five years. President Leguía could not deny the rejection of a part of the Legislative to the ratification and exchange of the document. Negative that also the population would make feel in 1932 when a group of Peruvians tried to vindicate the territory yielded to the native boson, without any success.

Politically and as expected, the result of the suffrage of August 4 and 5, 1929, revealed that the presidential mandate remained for a third term in the hands of Augusto B. Leguía. As the only candidate he obtained an overwhelming majority and the support of the members of both houses of Congress. However, the impact of the Wall Street crisis of 1929 showed the weaknesses of political alliances, whose members began to depart from the official party. To the suspension of work and the interruption of state resources was added the lack of payments with the North American and national financial institutions.

The conclusion of this period also allows us to contemplate the last presence of a religious and a military active as parliamentarians, the last being the presbyter Mariano García, deputy for Canas and Espinar from 1919 to 1924 and General César Canevaro, representative for Huancavelica and president of the Chamber of Senators in 1921, respectively.

The economic aspect of the 1920 Charter was complemented by the acts of the regime that reflected a liberal and exporting trend, which led to the modernization of the State with the participation of national capitals, but above all Americans within a development model of outside inward and that was reflected in the political speech of Augusto B. Leguía and in the corresponding laws: "On the coast irrigation, in the sierra, communication; in the jungle, I colonize. " Here again, it was a cultural policy imposed until the civilization of the inhabitants.

To achieve its mission, it increased taxes, increased public administration, but through its relations with the United States it secured loans and technical cooperation in agriculture, health and education. Situation that signified a considerable increase of the external debt in 221 million soles, equivalent to eight times the amount of the debt, at the beginning of its mandate.

The modernization generated the establishment of autonomous legal bodies oriented to the financial economic sector: The Central Reserve Bank, the National Collection Administration and the General Comptroller of the Republic. The Central Reserve Bank of Peru began its work on April 4, 1922, under the presidency of lawyer Eulogio Romero to have a monetary system that did not generate inflation especially in this regime that had a bonanza thanks to economic growth by new taxes and money from the United States of America.

In 1930, before the resounding fall of the regime, new conditions were created for the reorganization of the state and, above all, by influencing the regulation of the State in economic matters; that originally had as its purpose its recovery after the Wall Street world crisis of 1929. In that sense, the arrival in Peru of economist Edwin Kemmerer, heading the mission that bears his name during the provisional government of David Samanez Ocampo, established a series of measures that were fulfilled in the subsequent regimes until achieving in 1937 to have a surplus within responsible economic management.

IV. THE CONSTITUTION OF 1933 AND ITS IMPACT

The proposal of La Patria Nueva had revealed the transfer of power from the old civilist oligarchy to a new group (urban plutocrat), embodied by Leguía himself who later doubted whether he had represented the middle class: ...

through an excivilista who wore jaquet, was fond of horse racing ... (Guerra, 1994, Volume VIII, p.98).

The penetration of the United States, within the project of Peruvian governmental improvements (public and private sector: oil, mining, sugar, cotton, communications, etc.), provided the money that ended up being used as an instrument of political alliance. Fact that weakened the institutionality of the country to generate a degree of corruption until then not known. The wear of power of the Oncenio was of such magnitude that the President decided to transfer his powers to a Military Junta presided over by the former Minister of War, General Manuel María Ponce, who despite publicly announcing the resignation of the former president and the summons to a new National Assembly, had no echo.

From Arequipa, commander Luis Miguel Sánchez Cerro led the uprising that extended to Lima and replaced, through another military junta headed by himself, the short-lived government of Ponce. To this was added the installation of the National Sanction Court, an organ not contemplated in the Constitution of 1920 that had the mission to investigate and punish possible cases of corruption in contracts entered into on behalf of the State from July 4, 1919 until the fall of the regime. Another questionable aspect was the exploitation in the name of the law of road conscription and that of vagrancy.

In the external sphere, the celebration of the Treaty with Colombia was questioned, which removed Leticia from the national territory, as well as the degree of dependence of the Peruvian State against the United States. The popular support for the coup d'etat soon had the response of the Executive with the repeal of the law of roads. However, the other demands, as well as the recovery of the institutionality of the country, required the convening of elections for the President of the Republic and of a new Legislative, under the version of the Constituent Assembly with the participation of 120 representatives (Decrees Laws N No. 6953 and No. 6979).

In this interim, the argument of establishing a transitional regime composed of representatives of different regions of the country as long as the political entities regained leadership prevailed. Thus, Sanchez Cerro was replaced by the National Board of Government chaired by David Samanez Ocampo, which raised economic measures and issued the Statute of Elections through Decrees. It should also be noted the appointment of a commission chaired by Manuel Vicente Villarán, eminent jurist, with the aim of formulating a draft of the state constitution, which was presented at the beginning of the new term.

Víctor Raúl Haya de la Torre was presented by the Peruvian Aprista Party (APRA) and Colonel Luis Miguel Sánchez Cerro by the Revolutionary Union (UR), and the latter was declared winner by the National Jury of Elections, which allowed him to have 67 seats in the Assembly, sharing the mandate with 24 Aprista seats, to which were added others occupied by Decentralists, Socialists and independents, among which Víctor Andrés Belaúnde stood out. The presidential electoral contest reached borders of popular demonstration due to the charisma and extreme positions demonstrated by both candidates, which was accentuated, even more, with the difference of the result between the first and second candidate that reflected only 4 percent of the total valid votes.

The APRA as he did not want to accept the defeat and the country soon perceived the antagonism of these forces even within the Congress. He was elected Luis Antonio Eguiguren as president of the Congress, being accompanied by Clemente J. Revilla, former Civilist, deputy and senator until 1917, as vice president. On the same date, the new president of the Republic and his cabinet assumed functions. Meanwhile, the Legislature approved its Internal Regulation for the establishment of work commissions without inhibiting the control of the Executive, emphasizing that article that ordered the compulsory attendance of the ministers to the parliamentary precinct at the request of 24 representatives, a fact that caused discomfort in the regime that tried to modify it. Events in the north of the country and public criticism, through leaflets or newspaper articles, caused the Executive to send the draft of the emergency law for the maintenance of public order to the Assembly. The approved norm, under partisan criteria, established the legal use of control mechanisms when entrusting them to the Minister of Government and political authorities and leaving without effect the existence of precautionary principles of defense and legal security for the individual. The Judiciary and the guarantee of Habeas Corpus were left out of the system.

In use of the Internal Regulation, apristas and decentralistas representatives demanded the concurrence of the respective minister, fact that initiated the detention of every assembly member considered dangerous for the Executive, among them: Carlos Doig y Lora, Gustavo Neuhaus, Arturo Sabroso, Luis Alberto Sánchez , Carlos M. Cox, evidencing a palpable sample of the attack against the parliamentary immunity. The efforts of the president of the Legislative against the positions of the mayority of members of their own institution were in vain. By strategy, they preferred to leave aside the discussion about arbitrary measures to address other aspects of the country's life. Situation that ended up deepening more the convulsed climate and created the conditions for a civil war. In accordance with the emergency law, Martial Courts were established (Law No. 7546 of July 15, 1932), especially after taking the O'Donnovan Barracks in Trujillo.

In reference to the Villarán draft, the legislators who are members of the Constitution Committee made the changes and, as their work progressed, they were forced to show their agreements; taking a year for the final elaboration. The signing of the Constitution of 1933 was also the propitious moment to express through the reservations of some parliamentarians their concern for the recovery of the functions of control by the judiciary. The Congress reconstructed, in this theoretical framework, the democratic system with the introduction of political, economic and social guidelines in the new Charter. For this, he maintained the classical distinction of expressing a series of rights of individual character and showing the state organization with the distribution of powers where the preference was granted to the Legislative, which is known doctrinally as a dogmatic and organic part, respectively.

The Constitution of 1933 granted political leadership to Congress, in response to the leadership of the caudillo Augusto B. Leguía, generating control mechanisms for the President of the Republic. Which makes us perceive the lack of memory of the constituents with respect to previous political experiences. Finally, the agreement was reached to elect the president by popular direct suffrage, which would be proclaimed by the National Elections Board, under the premise of having obtained a simple majority no less than one third of valid votes (Article 138º).

In its absence, the Congress appointed the winner of the three candidates with the highest number of votes. In case of vacancy, the functions were referred to the Council of Ministers, the Legislative having to choose the replacement with the purpose of filling the position until the end of the mandate.

Despite coming to the conviction of imposing the mixed presidential-parliamentary regime, it lacked an integrated system that reflected true control. Emptiness and inaccuracies generated difficulties in its operation that only the casuistry would be responsible for solving. It was decided to grant a mediated role to the president of the Council of Ministers, to whom powers were assigned to which the Head of State depended to the point that without his authorization he could not appoint or remove the ministers. The political weight of the chief executive was subject to that of his collaborators, since he was able to carry out an administrative act without having the respective ministerial endorsement, otherwise the act lacked legal value. In order to link the political powers, it was decided that the ministers could be members of Congress, which did not exclude their being questioned and censured. Circumstances that raise the concern for the separation of power because indistinctly could be continued with the government line as a representative of the regime and then become its auditor as a member of the Legislature.

The novelty occurred with the conformation of the so-called Functional Senate that should represent the participation of the living forces and social institutions. According to Pareja (1944):

"A Parliament constituted by political elements ignores the economic and social realities of the country and does not facilitate the participation of living forces and institutions organized in the Government of the Nation" (p.203).

Although this intention was maintained, the legislators decided to create a transitory mechanism that ended up being permanent. On the other hand, the

Internal Regulation of the Congress did not make functional distinction between deputies and senators, reason for which we can consider that the institution of the functional or technical Senate, as such, did not take place. With regard to checks and balances between political bodies, the President of the Republic lacked the power to dissolve or delay the functioning of the Congress.

The constitutional control of the laws was also reserved, a mechanism that however was assigned to the magistrates according to the Preliminary Title of the Civil Code of 1936. Circumstance that would pose a conflict of competence and where the jurisprudence would be in charge of finding a way out by pointing out that the judges could only apply such control in cases of private law. On the other hand, the 1933 Charter, although it maintained the classification of guarantees in national, social and individual, innovated this matter by placing the individual and social rights under the protection of the habeas corpus remedy (Article 69). However, unlike the previous Charter stipulating, in its original version, that the guarantees could not be suspended by any authority, the Executive was granted discretion to do so when necessary for the security of the State (Article 70º).

The political situation that demanded the maintenance of an order led the legislators to establish the death penalty as well as the crimes of treason and maintain the homicide, all deriving from the legal regulation (Article 54) and in the same way the installation of special courts was expedited (article 229), which reveals that the Oncenio, despite being a dictatorship, was more cautious in maintaining, at least, theoretical legal approaches such as jurisdiction over civilians and military within the process of judgment. Regarding the use of property, the Charter was receptive to incorporate the concept of harmony with social interest (article 34); However, at the same time it persisted with the individualist spirit (Article 31), according to which each owner had the full disposition of the attributions of the good as such.

The Constitution also maintained the legal recognition of indigenous communities, stipulating that land would be procured for those who did not have sufficient extension according to their needs. For this purpose, land owned by individuals (articles 207 and 211) would be expropriated. Finally, decentralization was also addressed under the supervision of the Departmental Council, which would be established in the places indicated by the law, retaking the spirit and the old practices of the previous Letters. The climate of political instability unleashed in 1932 produced a series of irregularities on the part of the Revolutionary Union and the Popular Revolutionary American Alliance Party with a repression so violent that it fanned the frictions existing both in the city and in the countryside and had its point final in the murder of the then President of the Republic, General Luis Sánchez Cerro at Santa Beatriz Racetrack on April 30, 1933.

Faced with the impending power vacuum and the absence of the figure of the Vice President of the Republic, the Charter established the succession of power will rest in the Council of Ministers as a whole, calling elections in 30 days. Another alternative was for Congress to appoint a citizen to conclude the mandate of the ill-fated president. It was thus that the ex-civilian legislators who later formed the Unión Revolucionaria group opted for the appointment of General Oscar R. Benavides Larrea, an active military officer who was exempted from the impediments of being a military officer in order to assume the first magistracy. The Legislative, with a majority of the government party managed to keep the emergency law, given the current instability.

On one occasion, with Domingo García Belaunde we were members of the jury for the admission of new students of the Master's Degree in Constitutional Law of the Pontifical Catholic University of Peru and he asked me about the backstage of the death of Sánchez Cerro. I indicated that one of the previous passages had to do with their safety, since they had already attacked him in the district of Miraflores and it was a fact that something similar would happen when he went to the racetrack. The Emperor of Japan had given him a bulletproof vest that was bulky at the time and decided to try it while in the Government Palace. At that moment, "says Margarita Guerra M.," General Benavides was around. When he noticed the scene, he told the president that only the cowards wore a vest and he took his advice. To which García Belaunde added a testimony on behalf of the widow of Matías Manzanilla, who told him that the president died, his husband came swiftly to the palace and entered, finding General Benavides sitting in the presidential chair. Political curiosity.

The resignation of the cabinet Matías Manzanilla created the propitious moment so that Benavides adopted the position of appeasement and concord reflected in the law Nº 7782, granting a general amnesty and the court of the pending processes of political origin. In this way, the regime was characterized by being very personal, showing a tolerance with political forces such as APRA and the Communist Party, which led to a distancing with the members of the Congress of the Revolutionary Union caucus.

The APRA managed to infiltrate the high ranks of the army under the strategy that they propitiate the coup that would facilitate the rise of Haya de la Torre through new elections. Fact that was discovered and motivated the hardening in the relations between the regime and this political group. The experience of the assassination of President Sanchez Cerro motivated the reincorporation of the figures of the vice-presidencies, who in the same form and quality would substitute the Head of State, through the law Nº 8237 of April 1, 1936.

The elections of that year revealed the need to seek alliances between traditional parties that wished to continue in the political arena. In this way, the National Front appeared that grouped the Democrats, Reformist and Liberal Democrats; the Civil Party was supported by the National Agrarian and Nationalist Parties; and finally the Social Democratic Party had the support of the Popular Revolutionary American Alliance that sponsored Luis Antonio Eguiguren, as a candidate for the leadership of the Executive. This was imposed on the other opponents with the votes of APRA, which led to the annulment of these by the National Elections Board.

The Congress, supporting this measure and with the consent of its president Clemente Revilla, extended the mandate of General Benavides through Law No. 8463. The regime continued with its social policy but considered necessary the incorporation of constitutional measures through the popular consultation by plebiscite. Law No. 8929 included the approval of aspects of state regulation by said mechanism, which in the opinion of Benavides - decades ago - had been unconstitutional in the hands of Billinghurst.

The reforms eliminated the proportional representation system for minorities; expanded the mandate for deputies and senators to 6 years, renewing it every two years by lottery, pointing to this effect on July 28, 1941 and 1943. The so-called Functional Senate, until the guilds were recognized, would be composed by the Deparmental Representation. The presidential term was also extended to six years, beginning on July 28 of the year in which the respective elections would take place. Benavides rethinked the electoral timetable, leaving for the moment deferred the elections for President of the Republic and deputies. The congressional and Executive periods between 1939 and 1945, exceptionally, would begin on December 9, expiring on July 28, 1945. The members of the Senate would be elected by departments renewed by thirds on the same dates stipulated for Deputies.

On the eve of the renewal of representations during the year 1939, new conditions were presented for the elections of that year: on the one hand, the weakness of the traditional parties, the declaration of illegality of those considered leftist and the political erosion of the Revolutionary Union. Emerges the figure of Manuel Prado Ugarteche, who brought together industrialists, workers and the regime as it was considered. His option was addressed to the state intervention in the steel area and to the adoption of measures like those undertaken by Benavides that were destined to the majorities.

The following year with the situation of conflict in Europe and the recess of Congress, the latter granted the Executive through Law No. 9098 of May 9, 1940, the power to: ... dictate laws ... for the placement of our export products "(Planas, 1994, p.133), this being obliged to give account to its principal in the next session. To this it was added that the state agency entered a new sector of production with the creation of the Chimbote steel plant.

The renewal of power demanded the convening of general elections where José Luis Bustamante y Rivero, who took office on July 28, 1945, was imposed. Considered the author of Sanchez Cerro's manifesto during the 1930 Arequipa uprising, he headed a regime without a group own supported by independent and fundamentally in the APRA, with which there was no chemistry from the first year of the mandate. According to the Charter of 1933, the Legislative was the political center, which conditioned in practice the exercise of an increasing interference against the government that ended up establishing the "Parliamentary Dictatorship". As we know, the Peruvian constitutional tradition assigned the Chief Executive the power to organize his cabinet, a practice that in previous experiences had produced the rapprochement or distancing between the political forces represented in the congress.

Since 1945, the president wanted to retain the appointments of ministers, which led to the partisan use of controls on the Executive, such as interpellation and even ministerial censorship. Despite this situation, the APRA only came to censure the Minister Rómulo Ferrero Rebagliati, in the Treasury Portfolio. His presentation proposed an economic policy that did not satisfy the members of the Senate, which caused his resignation on October 3, 1945. At this juncture we also find the case of Agriculture Minister Enrique Basombrío Echenique, who was questioned by the representative of Chancay Alfredo Saco Miró Quesada, with the aim of informing the Chamber of Deputies about the increase of prices in food products, the control of these and the campaigns to be carried out to avoid hoarding. Asked if he knew the price of the pallares in the city of Ica, he demonstrated the opposite, which was not causal for the vote of censure to be resorted to, as in a distorted way it has been claimed:

"Ministers have fallen who have been censored in this same room for not knowing the price of the pallares in the market of Ica and this is not possible to admit in a country that wants to be serious" (Torres and Torres, 1993, volume II, p 1301).

The next day, said minister presented his resignation. Experience that motivates us reflection because it was governed for the party and not for the country, unless it had a card. The collegiate strategy was more oriented towards asserting its leadership protected by the promulgation of norms.

The next day, said minister presented his resignation. Experience that motivates us reflection because it was governed for the party and not for the country, unless it had a card. The collegiate strategy was more oriented towards asserting its leadership protected by the promulgation of norms.

Although the President of the Republic could block them through his observation, the constitutional system provided that the Legislature had the final say in promulgating it. An example of this was the tenor of law No. 10334 of December 29, 1945, which modified the plebiscitary reforms of the Benavides government. Between that date and 1947, the congress was held in different legislatures with a short pause between one and the other.

In 1948, the Chief Executive opened his cabinet made up of the military with the aim of recovering the political leadership he had claimed from the beginning, only that by then the social environment was between strikes, hoarding subsistence and repression. The right sought the assistance of the Minister of War, General Manuel Apolinario Odría Amoretti to head the coup d'état, a mechanism that allowed him to reach power on October 27 of the same year, displacing the Constitutional President of the Republic.

Subsequently this fact was institutionalized through Decree Law No. 10889 (November 2, 1948) the Military Government Junta was established and later Decree Law No. 10894 established the conditions for Odría to present himself as a presidential candidate. Legitimacy was necessary to continue in the government he demanded the call for elections in 1950, appearing for President of the Republic: General Ernesto Montagne for the National Democratic League and Manuel Odría for the Restorative Party. He took charge of capturing his opponent accusing him of conspiring with the proscribed apristas, with which to be single candidate ended up becoming the new Constitutional President of the Republic, achieving a majority in Congress.

In the beginning, the Executive devalued the currency by 41%, eliminated exchange controls, but maintained the increase in public spending. Although the regime was constitutional, the law of internal security remained, which limited the exercise of opposition parties. Under the motto of Health, Education and Work were reflected in the construction of hospitals and their equipment, the creation of the Social Assistance Center, comprehensive educational reform and the creation of the Ministry of Labor. The exploitation of oil carried out on the continental shelf in the northern part of the country led Congress to collect the doctrine of the 200 miles, previously proposed by Bustamante y Rivero in the respective Supreme Decree No. 781 of August 1, 1947.

The year of 1956 revealed its own wear of the regime evidencing an electoral conjuncture with the appearance of new political forces: the Christian

Democracy that supported Hernando de Lavalle, the Democratic Youth Front with Fernando Belaúnde Terry and the Pradista Democratic Movement (later called Peruvian)), whose candidate was Manuel Prado Ugarteche. The pradista offer to repeal Law No. 11049 Law of Internal Security of the Republic in exchange for APRA electoral support helped to establish the necessary conditions to face the elections on better terms (García Belaunde, 1979, 85). The APRA agreed with Prado and with it the steps for the so-called Coexistence stage (1956-1962) were given.

It is important to highlight the incorporation of women in political work. Law No. 12391 modified Article 84 of the 1933 Charter, which originally stated that citizenship only fell to men of legal age, those married at 18 years of age or those who were emancipated. The granting of the right of suffrage to women in 1955 not only expanded the electoral base but since then allowed the possibility that they would occupy the seats in the Legislative. In this way, it was possible the appearance of 9 legislators in the Congress:

In the Chamber of Deputies: Manuela Billinghurst López and Matilde Pérez Palacio, for Lima; Alicia Blanco Montesinos de Salinas and María Eleonora Silva Silva, for Junín; Lola Blanco de la Rosa Sánchez for Ancash, María de Colina de Gotuzzo for La Libertad, Carlota Ramos de Santolaya for Piura, Juana M. Ubilluz de Palacios for Loreto and Inés Silva de Santolalla as Senator for the department of Cajamarca (Congreso, 2000, pp. 489-494).

II. FORMAL CONSTITUTIONALISM AND COEXISTENCE 1956-1962

After scrutinizing the election results, it was determined that the apristas votes decided the return of Manuel Prado Ugarteche to the Presidency of the Republic and this one, once in the government, tried to preserve a profile according to the different political stores, fulfilling, for example, with one of them, the APRA, by returning it to the law. The results of the elections also showed the appearance of a new political leader, the ex-deputy for Lima, Fernando Belaúnde Terry, who came second in the elections. The Congress of this period was formed in its majority by the members of the Peruvian Democratic Movement and the APRA. The decision of Haya de la Torre to maintain Prado loyally was proved by the fact that the Apristas did not formulate a vote of no confidence during his second government. However, the fissures for the APRA party were inevitable after the dishonorable contrast of having an anti-oligarchical origin, gathered in its Minimum Program of the famous Discourse of Acho, to finally coexist with the oligarchy.

The agricultural crisis due to the drought demanded a new order in finance. Despite criticism from a sector of the right unhappy with the APRA presence, Manuel Prado invited Pedro Beltrán, well-known Peruvian liberal, to be finance minister. Beltrán was in charge of cleaning up the fiscal coffers without being able to oppose the approach of the regime, which decided to continue its strategy of intervention in the economy based on the thesis of the Economic Commission for Latin America (ECLAC):

"... there is no doubt that coercive planning would make Peru the worst damage imaginable. It would quickly lead to inflation, to the collapse of the currency, to the rising cost of living, to the unemployment of thousands of workers, to the decline in national income and income per person, to the flight of capital, to the generalization of misery and the formation of a corrupt clique that, on behalf of the State, would own the country "(Barrenechea, 1998, p.15)

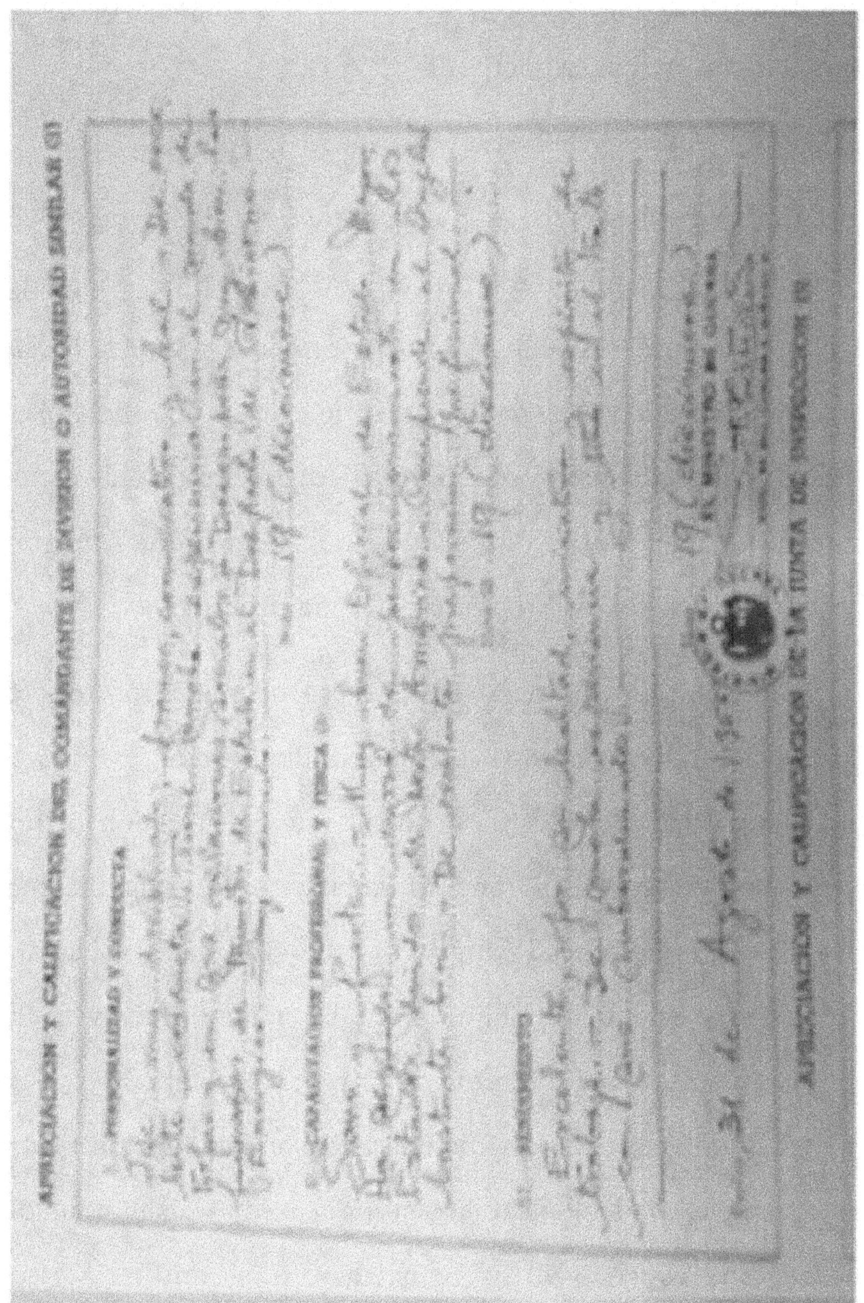

Qualification of the former minister after leaving to be incumbent
(Ministry of War. Lima, August 31, 1955)

Under the leadership of Prado, Law No. 13270 of the Industrial Promotion Law (November 30, 1959) was issued, granting incentives to the private sector to boost national manufacturing activity that still depended on imports. Three years later, at the State level, the National Planning Institute (INAP) was created to establish short, medium and long-term development priorities, a fact that was not seconded by future governments.

At the level of rights, the Congress approved by Legislative Resolution No. 13282 of December 15, 1959 that incorporated the Universal Declaration of Human Rights of 1948 into our legal system. Regarding housing needs and access to land, an inconclusive aspect of the previous regimes, President Prado tried to respond to this problem through the creation of the Commission for Agrarian Reform and Housing chaired by Pedro Beltrán. This concluded with the recommendation of the use of the lands in the area of the Amazon, as well as the cancellation of control over the prices of food products.

Regarding housing, the disappearance of lease payment controls for property owned by private individuals was considered, but at the same time it proposed the need for the State to direct its action to the construction of housing. The rapprochement between APRA and Manuel Prado during the mandate had made it foresee that the official support for the candidacy of Haya de la Torre for the Presidency of the Republic would be a fact. However, the electoral contest of 1962 also showed the reformist alternative embodied in the architect Fernando Belaúnde Terry, who by then had consolidated his party strength with a more pragmatic than ideological line, summarized in his famous phrase "Peru as a doctrine", and He enjoyed the sympathy of the middle class and even the army. Since May 26, 1962, the Armed Forces pointed out the presence of several irregularities in the elections of that year, highlighting the adulteration of the voter rolls for the suffrage, the double issuance of electoral books to apristas and pradistas, the existence of a number of votes greater than that of the voters and the interference of the political authorities in favor of a certain candidate in 10 departments (El Comercio, June 28, 1962).

The evidence was presented to the National Elections Panel, which dismissed it as reports. Although the electoral process gave Víctor Raúl Haya de la Torre a winner by only 13 thousand votes (Manrique 2009: p.232), he did not surpass the 33.33% constitutionally required to be proclaimed as the first president. In that case, according to article 138 of the Constitution of 1933, the definitive election was empowered to the Congress, at that time, of majority belonging to the Coexistence meadow-APRA now under the name Democratic Alliance. This determined that the military body reiterated its questioning of said process, demanding the annulment of the electoral body, but the latter refused. This situation ended with the coup d'état on July 17, 1962, behind which was the veto imposed on the APRA leader due to the events that took place in Trujillo in 1932. President Manuel Prado was deposed and declared in recess to the Legislative Power.

Unlike other organized raids, the 1962 Government Military Junta was of an institutional nature, with the participation of the different military corps, presided over by army Generals first Ricardo Pérez Godoy and then Nicolás Lindley, the Vice Admiral of the Navy. war Juan Francisco Torres Matos and the Major General of the air force Pedro Vargas Prada Peirano. In the environments of the legislative chambers, the commissions in charge of drafting the preliminary draft of the Electoral Statute were held: the Senators Planning Commission as well as the Permanent Deputies' Communications Board.

They were joined by the work carried out by the National Intelligence Service, which made a diagnosis of the causes of the conflicts in the southern highlands and, in general, the social unrest in the Andes of Peru. It is worth noting that the continental context is marked by the triumphant Cuban revolution 3 years before (1959) and the insurrectional projection that the exploited popular sectors and the radicalized middle sectors of Latin America face against the national oligarchies and their geopolitical subordination to the States United. Thus, the integral measures of the military diagnosis demanded that the governing Board recommend to the parties that they place in their government plans the way the Agrarian Reform would be carried out.

CHAPTER FIVE

De facto governments and the construction of the new democracy

I. THE ELECTORAL STATUTE OF 1962 AND THE RETURN TO FORMAL DEMOCRACY 1963-1968

For the general elections, the military junta enacted the Electoral Statute (Decree Law No. 14250) where it stipulated that the representations in the Chamber of Deputies were reduced from 182 to 145 seats (Echegaray, 1965, page 944), introducing the bases of the so-called distribution figure or D'Hont method, within a new electoral organization that highlighted the independence of the corresponding entity. The political forces were summarized in the APRA-UNO Coalition (apristas and Unión Nacional de Odriístas), also called the Super-coexistence, which had a majority in Congress, and the AP-DC Alliance (Popular Action and Christian Democracy), which it came to occupy the Executive.

In this way the government was led by Fernando Belaunde Terry as president of the Republic, accompanied by Edgardo Seoane Corrales and Mario Polar Ugarteche, first and second vice presidents of the Republic. The expectation was very high for the structural changes that had to be carried out, displacing the oligarchic dominion present after independence. Peasants, union organizations, student leaders and the middle class waited for the so-called "100 days" to see if the Belaunde regime faced the aspects whose solution was still postponed from previous mandates: the nationalization of the International Petroleum Company (IPC) that it exploited the oil in Talara, the Agrarian Reform to put an end to the latifundios and the easements, the decentralization of the State, the plans for popular housing, the support to the national industry, the tax reform and the regional redistribution of tax revenues.

Although the United States punished the new regime with the freezing of international loans for the alleged interventionist measure against the IPC; However, between 1962 and 1965, the Central American Intelligence Agency (CIA) supported the defeat of the guerrilla actions of the National Liberation Army (ELN) led by Héctor Béjar, Javier Heraud and Juan Pablo Chang, for the Peruvian Armed Forces

Regarding the Agrarian Reform, this was given experimentally in those convulsed areas located in the southeast of the country, such as La Convencion or Paucartambo in Cusco where the recovery of land by the indigenous peasants led by Hugo Blanco or Saturnino Huillca, among many others, forced the government in 1963 to a first reformist action. The Agrarian Reform by then already appeared in political debates as "a solution to modernize the Peruvian agriculture and alleviate the misery of the Andean peasants" (Contreras and Cueto 2000: p.298). Later, Law No. 15037 laid the groundwork for an application at the national level, where upon evaluation, the State expropriated the lands of individuals to adjudicate them to the peasants. The first procedure of expropriation of a large estate for the sake of Agrarian Reform in the history of Peru had not ended even after five years of the enactment of the law. In practice, these lands ended up being the surplus or those not used, so the adoption of weak measures did not disappear the consolidated latifundio since the early twentieth century. Obtaining greater reform via the Legislative was difficult if the majority representation was oppositional, having among its ranks latifundistas like Julio de la Piedra del Castillo.

There was also a contradiction in the Constitution, between Article 34 that raised the use of goods in harmony with the social interest while the 31st picked up the individualistic spirit with which each owner had the full disposition of the attributions of the good as such, leaving aside the agreement with the social interest postulated by Pope Leo XIII in the Encyclical Rerum Novarum.

The oligarchy questioned the agrarian reform of the regime arguing the inviolable character of the property, but above all rejecting the deferred payment in annual redemption armadas, since the treasury did not have the necessary resources for immediate payment. In that sense, the Armed Forces perceived that the reform mechanism lacked a constitutional effectiveness that would take them forward and that this vacuum could be used by the leaders of those convulsed zones, defeated years ago.

In turn, the presidential weakness to impose agrarian reform against the oligarchy exceeded social tolerance by nesting the conditions to relaunch the guerrilla war in 1965 by the Movimiento de Izquierda Revolucionaria (MIR), led by Luis Felipe De la Puente Uceda , and the ELN in Peru, however, the Peruvian government, advised by the CIA infiltrated in the direction of the MIR, as the historian Nelson Manrique Gálvez (2013) maintains, would bomb them until they were crushed militarily.

The Belaunde regime considered that the military repression was not gravitating, error that was taken advantage of by the APRA to reinforce its leadership established in the Legislative through votes of censorship. The AP-DC Alliance resorted to the formation of cabinets with the presence of parliamentarians, a practice rehearsed years ago, to avoid censure by the majority of the opposition. The Congress led by the APRA-UNO Coalition oversaw stopping the discussion about the initiatives coming from the government, either postponing them, introducing important alterations in the proposals or imposing them.

Unlike the 1945 experience where both the Government and Congress belonged to the National Democratic Front, from which there was a distancing between the members of the same political force, the correlation of forces in 1963 showed the presence of two antagonistic forces. Each one wanted to prevail its political leadership: an example of this is found in the convocation to an extraordinary legislature that met for seven months. A balance of the measurement of forces reveals how the AP-DC Alliance was forced to form six ministerial cabinets where censorship was addressed to ministers individually.

Although this power dispute came to halt the implementation of the reforms that had already encountered obstacles from the beginning, did not persuade the President of the Republic to call the people to electorally break the impasse of the system.

Both the APRA and the left benefited at this juncture because the constitutional powers (Article 123, paragraph 5 of the 1933 Charter) provided members of the Legislative with the possibility of introducing expenses on a partisan basis in reference to the problems closest to the settlers, which demonstrated the effectiveness and speed of their work, a fact that did not exclude the highlight of their partisan character. Also, the impossibility of reformism led Popular Action militants to resign to create or register in left-wing political stores.

The Alliance thanks to its supporters in the capital won the mayor's office in Lima with Luis Bedoya Reyes (1964-1970).

The ministers immolated before the parliamentary censorship.
BNP Hemeroteca, Caretas No. 320, October 26 - November 5, 1965, p. 69

However, Belaunde's rugged governance was felt with the presence of the economic crisis, which in 1965 had been a reflection of the stagnation of exports, increase in imports, the increase in public spending generated by the implementation of reforms and the reduction of fiscal resources. US pressure condemned President Belaunde's regime to arrange loans with private entities. Its management was punished by the electorate, on November 13, 1966 with the complementary elections for legislators when the Coalition obtained greater votes than the Alliance, being those issued in the provinces. Here the management of the economic policy was the occasion to continue with the ministerial censorship while the Executive did not take into account the members of the Coalition as their future ministers.

The proposals of Pedro Beltrán to reduce public treasury spending consisting in terminating the industry subsidy and devaluing the currency were not taken into account until 1967 when the regime was forced to make them prioritize the devaluation. The following year, the attrition had been such that the president had to arrange the formation of his new cabinet with independent sympathizers of APRA, giving birth to the so-called "Cabinet Conversado" under the direction of Oswaldo Hercelles García. This fact motivated the withdrawal of the Christian Democracy from the Alliance. Politically this was the occasion to constitute a platform that would allow APRA to reach power in the 1969 elections. Under the authorization of extraordinary measures, the government issued in two months measures considered populist by Supreme Decree 287-68 / HC: decreased spending of the State, refinanced its international debt, reformulated the tax system with direct and indirect taxes, satisfied wage demands and accentuated state participation in the economy, reflected in its 29 companies that were part of the State's Business Activity.

However, the critical issue was still related to the nationalization of the IPC, a US enclave in Peruvian territory. Suddenly in the message to the Nation of that year, the first president announced the solution to the litigation of La Brea y Pariñas "without the State having to pay for the soil, the subsoil, or the facilities" (Guerra Martinière, 1994, volume IX, p. 52).

The North American company still remained with the Talara refinery, enjoying the monopoly of gasoline, to which was added the delivery of one million hectares in the jungle. The details of the negotiation were stipulated in the so-called Acta de Talara, which on page 11 indicated the price of the sale of crude oil from the Fiscal Petroleum Company to the US oil company.

The disappearance of this page led to the resignation of the board chairman of this entity, who later on in a televised address made public the loss in mention, generating the political scandal (Pease, 1974, p.11), preamble of the interruption of the presidential mandate.

The following months aggravated the situation with the appearance of corruption manifestations, the entry of contraband by members of the Armed Forces and the departure of militants of the official party, among which was Edgardo Seoane Corrales, first Vice President of the Republic who decided to create Socialist Popular Action (also known as Seoanista) with Gustavo Mohme Llona: The Party is divided into two that in practice was identified more with the characters than with the doctrine:

... justifying the rupture of his Party, the President affirms that the names of Acción Popular and Belaúnde are synonyms (Pease, 1974, p.14).

The situation of crisis created the conditions for the irruption of the Armed Forces, the same one that occurred on October 3, 1968 with General Juan Francisco Velasco Alvarado, then president of the Joint Command of the Armed Forces. This unconstitutional break revealed the contradictions that had arisen within the State, the struggle between its political organs, but also the lack of response to popular expectations that had pinned their hopes on the reformist measures. It was necessary to reorder the constitutional aspect with the consequent distribution of the powers of the Executive and the Legislative under the idea of achieving a balance of forces, whose benefit would redound in the country and avoiding solutions that as a palliative would only respond to electoral interests.

II. THE STATE REFORMS OF THE REVOLUTIONARY GOVERNMENT OF THE ARMED FORCES (GRFA) AND THE CONSTITUTION OF 1979

After the coup d'état, the Revolutionary Government of the Armed Forces (Gobierno Revolucionario de las Fuerzas Armadas) raised many expectations about both its performance and its permanence. The oligarchy imagined it as the beginning of a year similar to that of the Military Junta of 1962. However, the military intervention carried out six days later on the oil installations of Talara, controlled then by the International Petroleum Company owned by the multimillion-dollar American family Rockefeller, granted the regime sympathies for the nationalism deployed and unprecedented popular support. Although from the beginning it was pointed out that the expropriation carried out would not have a consideration, six years later the Secret De la Flor Agreement - Greene showed that the Peruvian State would pay 76 million dollars. In 1969, the military government headed by General Velasco Alvarado created the state company Petróleos del Perú, better known as Petroperú, to operate the oil industry with its own personnel and to supply the national demand for fuel.

Government intervention on oil and later on land, is circumscribed in the social function of the State as a historical response to the republican empirical future of Peru, according to the historian Jorge Basadre. The proposal of the regime was expressed in a planned economy, collected in the Ideological Bases of the Peruvian Revolution, which:

"... will lead to promote the role of state property for the benefit of the entire national community within the new organization of the Participatory State" (GRFA, 1975, p.11).

This participation, which already came to a small degree from previous governments, led the State to intervene progressively in economic activity through public companies, which would be over-dimensioned in the twelve years that the military regime would last. Even before the Revolutionary Government there were 29 and after it reached 192 registered, considering some of them as strategic: telephony, electricity, water, military weapons, etc., which is why they were unsaleable. This situation will change twenty-five years later (1993) when the notion of a strategic company will be re-elaborated and public companies will be submitted to market logic, privatizing them.

The next government measure was directed to the land issue, whose large areas were owned by the oligarchy, giving rise to the final agrarian reform (Decree Law No. 17716 Agrarian Reform Law) that replaced its similar from the government of Meadow. With it ended not only large estates or large tracts of land in a few hands but also bondage or free labor associated with the exploitation of peasants by landowners or gamonales. The agrarian reform was born with the collective action of the indigenous peasantry in the valley of La Convención in Cusco and manages to become an unstoppable demand for social justice that runs through the country.

The Armed Forces, disappointed with Belaunde and faced with the possibility of a revolutionary solution like the Cuban one in Peru, decide to execute anti-oligarchic, nationalist and even anti-imperialist measures. The agrarian reform was coined in a historical phrase pronounced by General Velasco: "Peasant, the boss will no longer eat your poverty". This measure displaced the individual property to prioritize the property of the workers, under the regime of the Agricultural Cooperatives of Production (CAPS) and the Agricultural Companies of Social Interest (SAIS).

However, the vertical implementation of this conception of agrarian reform did not satisfy the mobilized indigenous peasantry because, according to Hugo Blanco "(...) in practice the only beneficiaries were bureaucrats placed from above by the government (via) a system of bureaucratic cooperativism imported (without considering) the democratic communal tradition of our millennial ayllu". This disagreement, together with other reasons, weakened the administration of these entities without being able to maintain the national production of sugar and cotton, forcing the State to a permanent subsidy until the 1990s. Although Habeas Corpus appeals were filed in defense of the property, they did not proceed because the legal system at that time did not provide for the control of the law by the Judicial Branch.

Peruvian society before and after the coup d'état of the Armed Forces led by Velasco achieved unprecedented degrees of social mobilization to the point that trade unions and professional unions are created massively, peasant federations, student organizations, business associations, revolutionary parties, among others. Peru lives, almost 150 years later, a change of epoch that should have occurred with its independence. The Catholic Church is also forced to change via a new theology, the Theology of Liberation and the preferential option for the poor, where the Peruvian Gustavo Gutiérrez Merino is its maximum national exponent since 1971.

Apart from the reforms undertaken, it was complemented with others related to the cultural field that were again imposed. In this way, military advisers promoted the Law of Native Communities and Agricultural Promotion of the Selva and Ceja Regions of the Amazon, of June 24, 1974, which put into practice the legal anthropology of the time. The resolution of disputes, for minimum amounts or faults, was adjudicated in the first place to the communities themselves, whose resolution was in the nature of res judicata. As Galvez Revollar points out:

"... the pressures exerted by the natives themselves animated by the Amazonian vicariates imbued some by the actions of the Second Vatican Council and the enthusiasm of social scientists, working for the state, sensitized by the declaration of the" liberation of the indigenous of the Declaration of Barbados, 1971 "(2001, p.285).

To this is added, the establishment of Quechua as the official language, on May 27, 1975 (Decree Law No. 21156) to claim the largest indigenous people of Peru historically postponed, however, there was difficulty in its implementation as it was a written and spoken language. it differed according to the regions, for example, Cajamarca, Huaraz, Ayacucho and Cusco. For this reason, it was necessary the presence of experts to unify the language, a fact that was complemented with the application of the law of telecommunications and its similar that allowed the radio and television signals bilingual news. Actions that denoted innovations in the change of social and legal pluralism but that in the minds of the legislators of 1978 would not find echo, perhaps because they were produced by the Revolutionary Government.

Another reform was aimed at affecting ownership to move from a private to a participatory conception among workers, employers and shareholders. From this we would speak of the intervention of workers in the co-ownership and co-management of industrial companies thus forming industrial communities. Based on the Encyclical Letter Rerum Novarum "On the situation of the workers" of the Catholic Pope Leo XIII the worker was recognized not only his work through payment but also his permanence that was translated into continuity. This is how labor actions appear for years of service, which would also allow the presence of workers in the company's board of directors. This measure was complemented by the incorporation of the Social Property Companies (Decree Law No. 20598) and with a new type of legal entity organization: ... constituted within the principle of solidarity, for the purpose of carrying out economic activities "(article 1st). This is how the Social Law was born with a teleological interpretation that worked in favor of the individual in accordance with society. Authors such as Luis Bustamante Belaunde, Fernando de Trazegnies Granda, Jorge Avendaño Valdez and the young Carlos Blancas Bustamante bet on this new design of Law.

The march of the military revolution was affected by the economic recession due to the costs of the reforms, the health of the Head of State who already had a leg amputated and finally an altercation among the military high command, such as the Director of the Civil Guard and the Head of the Military House, who unleashed the police strike of February 5, 1975, concluding in the decision of the general commanders of each institute to appoint General Francisco Morales Bermúdez Cerrutti, grandson of the president Remigio Morales Bermúdez, as the new president of the Republic, on August 29 of that year. The new regime inaugurated the second phase, of right-wing tendency.

In this new phase there was a reorientation of the reforms, eliminating the existing ones without generating their replacements, for example, the National System of Social Mobilization (SINAMOS) was dismantled, whose budgetary allocation reached to the war. The second phase took distance from sectors of the left and proposed an approach to civility, as was pointed out in the Tupac Amaru Plan. Thus, on July 28, 1977, the President of the Republic convoked Elections for the Constituent Assembly, which:

"... will have as its exclusive purpose the draft of the new Political Constitution of the State, which will contain, among other things, the provisions that institutionalize the structural transformations that the Revolutionary government of the Armed Forces is carrying out." (Decree Law No. 21949, article 2).

This measure was not alien to the impact of the general strike that paralyzed the country demanding the return to democracy. The need for a new Charter required the president to hold prior meetings with the leaders of the political parties with the largest membership. The experience of the military government with the participation of advisors from different disciplines would motivate changes in the new state structure to be drawn up, such as the implications of the alleged Social Law, which, although it would disappear, would make its dimensions addressed to legal matters of a nature constitutional, civil, criminal, procedural and administrative. Added to this were the human rights summarized in the dignity of the human being, the pure theory of Kelsen's Law exposed in 1948 by Jorge Patrón Yrigoyen, the Peruvian constitutional tradition and the Spanish constitutional influence consigned in the 1978 draft Constitution of Spain whose copy would deliver months later King Juan Carlos I to the president of the Constituent Assembly, Víctor Raúl Haya de la Torre.

Parallel to the convocation, the government decided to reduce the age of majority to 18 for new citizens, preserving the requirement of being literate for both sexes as well as registering with the National Elections Board. (Decree Law No. 21994, of November 15, 1977). In this way, the electoral population of voters was 4'966,016 according to the JNE, who voted 4'173,561 (84.05%), considering the valid votes whose number was 3'511,895 (84.16%)

The Peruvian Aprista Party won the elections reaching 1'241,174 votes (35.39% of valid votes), followed by the Popular Christian Party with 835,294 votes (23.78%) and by the Popular and Popular Peasant Workers Front with 433,413 (12.34%), between many other political groups of the left. On the other hand, the preferential vote was imposed, allowing not only to elect the political party but also the ideal candidate: thus breaking the tradition by which only the first numbers of each list benefited. This option replaced the designations of each political group lacking primary elections where the high party leadership was the one that finally made the decision at the time of making the lists. This form of vote generated distrust in a certain political force:

"... arguing that the military dictatorship wanted to divide the vote of this party grouping and thereby prevent its leader Víctor Raúl Haya de la Torre from obtaining the biggest vote". (ONPE-CIE, 2005, p.12)

This modality made the most voted candidate of the most voted party the new president of the Legislative Power, creating a tradition that since then has reflected the sympathy of the electorate. This collegiate was formed by a hundred constituents, who alternated the politicians of the Old Guard as Victor Raul Haya de la Totrre, Luis Bedoya Reyes, Genaro Ledesma Izquieta, Roberto Ramirez del Villar, Luis Alberto Sanchez, Hugo Blanco Galdós, César Vizcarra Vargas (father of the president Martín Vizcarra) with those of the new batch like

Alan García Pérez, Xavier Barrón Cebreros, Enrique Chirinos Soto, etcetera. They were granted a period of one year for the drafting and approval of the new Charter that would end on July 12, 1979, leaving its promulgation to the new government that was elected from the following elections. The president of the Assembly was very clear about the procedure:

"Our Constitution must emancipate itself from imitations and copies, without neglecting the universal legacy of political science. We need a concise and pragmatic Constitution that focuses on man and human rights and forges a new State for a better society "(PERU 1989, p.17)

Parallel to this, the military government, on behalf of the Peruvian State, signed the American Convention on Human Rights (Pact of San José) on July 28, 1978 (Decree Law No. 22231) with which Peru was ascribed to the supranational body of mandatory character both in the protection and in the defense of Human Rights.

III. NEOCOSTITUTIONALISM: THE COVENANT OF SAINT JOSEPH AND THE NEW VISION OF FUNDAMENTAL RIGHTS

To the constitutional model of the expressed rights, coming from French formation and from the 19th century, those that came from the interpretation of the Judicature were added, known as the non-expressed or unnamed. This is because the Pact of San José not only conjugated the legal tradition of the Roman-Germanic model typical of Spanish-speaking countries but also the Anglo-Saxon model of countries such as the United States, Canada, Belize, Bahamas, Barbados, Jamaica and Guyana and the Lusitanian model of countries such as Brazil, all in the understanding that law is a cultural product and houses different mechanisms that regulate social life. The Peruvian system, for example, incorporated the constitutional guarantees or protective mechanisms, such as habeas corpus (Constitution 1920), popular action (Letter of 1823) or amparo action, within a model that progressively established the so-called Constitutional Justice.

The time was propitious to establish a new Rule of Law, which, although incipient, postulated the unrestricted defense of fundamental rights whose statements came from international treaties and declarations, mostly from the United Nations, and would be incorporated into the drafting of the Constitution, which since then assumed its hierarchy as the supreme legal and political norm. We must also indicate that there was not a single valuation among the constituents of the international instruments in defense of rights, as we corroborate the minutes of the 26th Session of the Constitution and Regulation Commission, of March 13, 1979, when it was discussed whether or not the UN Declaration was a source of law, this was motivated by the opinion of the legislator Mario Polar who argued that beyond the document should protect the inherent faculties of the person:

"Human rights include natural rights, inalienable, which mean common political goals for all parties, aspirations that are not going to be done overnight, but progressively and that is why there is a provision expressed in the General Provisions. So, if this statement expresses a set of aspirations, I do not know why we're not going to mention them there. These are goals that we are setting ourselves for future political action "(Comisión Principal, 1978-79: Volume IV, p. 423).

The interest of the legislators to protect the individual from any arbitrary or usurping measure led Enrique Chirinos Soto to propose the following statement:

"The enumeration of the rights recognized in this chapter does not exclude others that the Constitution guarantees, nor others of a similar nature or that derive from the dignity of man, from the principle of sovereignty of the people, from the democratic state of law and from the republican form of government "(Comisión Principal, 1978-79: Volume V, page 313).

Another element that set a precedent was, at the initiative of Javier Valle Riestra González Olaechea, the establishment of the Court of Constitutional Guarantees following the Spanish model with the mission of guaranteeing the normative development of the country in keeping with the Constitution. With this initiative it was sought that this Court was the only entity that could act as a negative legislator, that is, by withdrawing a rule from the system challenged as unconstitutional. At the same time, the Judicial Power was empowered to participate in the constitutional control, in which case it could only be applied to the complaining party because it lacked the power to do so for all.

In the past, circumstances had already arisen where the law contradicted the constitutional articles and no contradiction was generated since in French thought the supreme norm was the law and not the Constitution. In this erratic way, lawyers had been trained in our country for decades. Finally, the Convention in its article 25 established the judicial protection of human rights.

IV. THE CONSTRUCTION OF THE DEMOCRATIC AND SOCIAL STATE

The participatory policy undertaken by the Revolutionary Government made it possible for the measures of inclusion for the time to count with greater speed, although these in practice did not always find the expected spirit of change. In fact, many of its beneficiaries ended up distorting the purposes and discrediting the benefits to society. A legitimate discussion but given in the middle of a de facto government and with the presence of renowned legislators.

Previously, since the early sixties, the doctrine of the people had penetrated the rural and urban sectors, demanding the participation without distinction of the settlers in the public life of the country. The presence of a State that does represent them was necessary. There were also still new rules that would bring the State closer to the settlers. Democracy in Peru was formal, not material, insofar as it was an exclusive institutional order for the privileged sectors, the elites, and exclusive for the popular and middle sectors, the peoples. For that reason, the reference in abstract to the democracy was perceived like a defense of the privileges to the detriment of a material democracy. The certain thing is that the political organization corresponded to all, although they did not invoke it.

On the one hand, the placing of the Constitution as a democratic political norm and as a supreme legal norm constituted the first step to assess the constitutional culture in the country, however, it was still necessary to shape the Peruvian mentality to bring the real powers closer to the people. Powers, towards a commitment to the constitutional State that goes beyond the legal State. The change irradiated, also, challenges the non-privileged sectors to a participation that breaks and exceeds unconditional assistance, which goes beyond any client relationship.

On the other hand, the constituent legislature postulated that, exceptionally, the shift system could legislate on certain matters with prior authorization of the Legislature through a standard with the status of a law called legislative decree, thus configuring the legal system of the time according to the Constitution. Before imposed decisions, the new tendency was the agreement, which did not settle among the settlers, as it occurs in other States, being more a mockery than an institutionality.

Culturally, the first phase of the military regime supported by professionals had gradually included and under its command Quechua as the official language, the communal jurisdiction as a special jurisdiction for the jungle and mountain areas and social media as ways to get closer to this idiomatic and legal pluralism. Faced with this, the constituent legislators had different approaches in this regard. The representative of the Workers', Peasants', Students' and Popular Front (FOCEP), Ernesto Sánchez, known as the Jilguero del Huascarán, proposed in the 37th session of the Constituent Assembly:

"Castellano is the official language of Peru. Quechua, Aymara and the different languages constitute national heritage. The State respects the peculiarities of each zone in which they have official use". (Comisión ¨Principal 1978, Volume VI, p. 121).

Genaro Ledesma and Jorge del Prado, both from the ranks of the left, affirmed the advantage of using the Quechua language to incorporate millions of Peruvians into a scheme that still privileged Spanish within the actions undertaken by the State (procedures, lawsuits, documents, etc). To this was added, the declaration of the Aymara and other languages with the same recognition. In the opinion of Enrique Chirinos Soto, these languages would be official in the district where they spoke. In the opinion of Enrique Chirinos Soto, these languages would be official in the district where they spoke. Ideas that were embodied in Article 83 of the 1979 Charter.

A theme related to the language was the delivery of justice in communal areas that was advanced since 1974. In this regard, legislators closed ranks stating that the formal system of legal monism should be respected because that was already defined since the nineteenth century. With this, the opportunity to deepen the institutional recognition of legal pluralism and complementary legal systems that could have helped resolve everyday conflicts in rural areas was lost.

Justice has been the cornerstone of coexistence in every society and was not an exempt issue within the measures set out by the Revolutionary Government of the Armed Forces through Decree-Law No. 1806. Thus, on December 23, 1969, the judicial branch was declared a reorganization and the members of the Supreme Court were dismissed. The new appointments would be made through the National Council of Justice composed of two delegates from the Executive Branch, two from the Legislative Branch, two from the Supreme Court, one from the Federation of Lawyers, one from the Lima Bar Association, one from the Academic Program of Law of the University of San Marcos and one of the Academic Program of Law of the universities of the country. This Council became operational on May 7, 1970, proceeding to elect judges and prosecutors.

He chose the magistrates of the candidates proposed by the Judicial Power, the Federation of Lawyers and the Bar Association, respectively. The norm empowered the new member to evaluate and punish judges and prosecutors without considering measures in case they contravened the spirit of the regime.

In those years, Dr. Vicente Ugarte del Pino, Dean of the Lima Bar Association, maintained an ironclad demand for independence from the Judiciary, a circumstance that caused him a series of slander and insults for daring to question this process, which he demonstrated as an innovator and of social justice, he believed in the lack of credibility of the Judiciary, even more so when the members of the National Council of Justice depended on a more political than legal designation.

This magistrate at the end of the sixties had postulated the existence of the National School of Magistracy, similar to that existing in European countries, under the concern that not only should judges and prosecutors be elected but also train them for a efficient performance of the judicial career (Ugarte, 1978, 622). The revolutionary experience was then reflected in the drafting of the new Charter of 1979 as the National Council of the Magistracy, with a design that included only lawyers led by the National Prosecutor (position created in 1856) and composed of representatives of the Court Supreme, one of the Federation of Lawyers, one of the Bar Association of Lima, two representatives of the Faculties of Law.

With this advice we appreciate the establishment of autonomous bodies of the justice system that will be incorporated into the constitutionalism and that were added to others of an economic nature coming from the management of the Leguía regime: The Central Reserve Bank, the National Collection Administration and the Comptroller's Office General of the Republic.

We must emphasize that in addition to the Court of Constitutional Guarantees and the National Council of Magistrates, the Public Ministry was added. Since the creation of the Real Audiencia de Lima by the New Laws (1542-1543), the highest instance of the administration of viceregal justice, judges and prosecutors had belonged to the same institution. Tradition that will continue with the establishment of the Peruvian State and will survive until 1979 when the Public Ministry is created, an autonomous institution of the justice system. Years before, the Organic Law of the Judicial Power of 1963 proposed a greater identification of prosecutors with the exercise of criminal action and made the variation in the name of Public Prosecutor's Office. This constituent creation promoted ex officio or at the request of a party the action of justice in defense of legality, citizen rights and public interests; acting also "... as an ombudsman before the public administration." Attribution that would materialize at the time of the internal armed conflict with the issuance of Resolution No. 92-89-MP-FN, of April 27, 1989, which created the so-called Special Prosecutor's Office in charge of the affairs of the Ombudsman's Office and Human Rights, under the responsibility of the prosecutor Clodomiro Chávez Valderrama.

The Revolutionary Government of the Armed Forces was in possession of a new Constitution, expedited for its entry into force, but also an economic situation characterized by constant readjustments, also known as "paquetazos", authored by the then Economy Minister Javier Silva Ruete.

V. THE RETURN OF FORMAL DEMOCRACY AND TERRORISM IN PERU REAL

Summoned the elections in 1980, the alliance AP-PPC (Popular Action and Popular Christian Party) was winning both in the Congress, where it obtained a majority, and in the Executive, where the architect Fernando Belaunde Terry became president of the Republic, for a second time.

The Peruvians of the urban and mainly coastal areas had expectations in the functioning of the democratic institutions, especially if the first act of the president would be the promulgation of the 1979 Constitution on July 28, 1980. The new period inherited a country in two. dimensions, formal Peru, of the existing political class focused on administering the Peruvian State, and real Peru, of the original migrant peoples from the countryside to the city who are objectors of the political class and the legitimacy of the Peruvian State. In addition, Belaunde would have to assume the economic liabilities of the military government at the same time as the beginning of the armed actions of Marxist and Maoist insurrectional groups. This context was permanent from Fernando Belaunde Terry (1980-1985), Alan García Pérez (1985-1990) to Alberto Fujimori (1990-1992).

The costs of the reforms added to the productive decline, the paquetazos and the establishment of a new tributary model incubated the protests, the informality, the violence and the internal armed conflict, marked by the terrorism of groups and the State terrorism leaving between the civil population. The new constitutionalism faced its first challenges in maintaining an adequate level of human dignity, in the absence of state protection or defenses of civil society organizations or political parties. The social mobilization and then the events that occurred in Ayacucho forced the regime to grant power to restore order to the Armed Forces to neutralize any type of alteration, which would materialize in the month of December 1982, comprising the departments of Ayacucho, Huancavelica and Abancay This action provoked the maximum number of indigenous persons disappeared in the country committed by the Armed Forces between 1980 and 2000 and the systematic commission of crimes against humanity, according to the Final Report of the Truth and Reconciliation Commission (2003).

The erosion of Belaunde's power inclined in 1985 the electoral preference to the Peruvian Aprista Party with Alan García Pérez at the head, who would become President of the Republic. It is anecdotal that this party since 1932 with Victor Raul Haya de la Torre as a historical leader was excluded from the official mandate on different occasions and even in 1963 that being a tenth of a percentage of the presidential chair and passing the final election to Parliament took place a coup d'etat to stop him. The APRA had congressional representation in the periods when they were not persecuted. His measures mainly oriented to the welfare of the majorities also sought to control the work of the government, but under a passionate and destructive criticism as we can see in the interpellations and censures of the ministers of Fernando Belaunde in his first term of 1963-1968. Before the death of Haya de la Torre in 1979, the crisis was generated by the succession among close relatives Luis Townsend Ezcurra and Armando Villanueva del Campo, with the second being preferred by the bases. This one postulated for president of the Republic, but it did not achieve its mission since his wife was Chilean. Later, Townsend would be separated from the party by denouncing "ideological deviation and signs of corruption", then forming his own group: The Haya Base Movement. Scenario that together with other factors gradually allowed Alan García Pérez at 35 years old to be president of Peru.

Again, the population had a lot of expectation not only for the youth of the president but also for his role as an opposition party because now he was becoming a government party for the first time. The 1979 Constitution, authored by the parties Aprista Peruano, Popular Cristiano and various leftist formations (although the latter decided not to sign it) would be put into practice. The context preceding Alan Garcia forced him to respond to expectations about economic policy with people. His inexperience and theft in the government led us to a historical hyperinflation worldwide.

The events that took place on June 18 and 19, 1986, while the celebration of the XVII Congress of the Socialist International took place, show the repression of the State in its maximum degree of State terrorism against the rioting in San Juan Baptist prisons in El Frontón island, San Pedro (San Juan de Lurigancho district) and Santa Bárbara (Chorrillos district) at a time when the workers' strike of the National Union of Penitentiary Workers (SINTRAP) began, a fact taken advantage of by the militants subversives of Sendero Luminoso that already had control in prisons. This measure was justified by Supreme Decree No. 006-86-JUS signed by the then Minister of Justice Luis Gonzales Posada, who declared the prisons as "restricted military zones", a circumstance that prevented the entry and presence of any civil authority.

The terrorist crimes of Sendero Luminoso and the Tupac Amaru Revolutionary Movement were complemented by the state crimes of García's government against the indigenous peasants. From the political apparatus of the same Aprista government, contradictions were even appreciated, it is enough to read the words of President García himself pronounced in the VII Aprista Youth Congress:

"We must recognize how Shining Path has active militants, dedicated, sacrificed. Wrong or not, criminal or not, the Senderista has what we do not have: Mistical Loyalty. Those people deserve our respect and personal admiration because they are, whether they like it or not, they are militants. " Ayacucho, May 22, 1988¨ (SOMOS, 2012, p.26).

The progressive distrust of the regime and the system allowed the emergence of leaders from different spheres of society known as the outsiders, who built the political forces around them. This circumstance evokes the fragility of the traditional political parties: Popular Action, Popular Christian Party, the Party, Peruvian Aprista and the Christian Democracy, which had come to govern. Characters such as Ricardo Belmont Casinelli (radio-television entrepreneur), Susana Díaz Díaz (artist), Alberto Fujimori Fujimori (engineer, former rector of the Agrarian University) and Mario Vargas Llosa (connoted writer) became a reflection of this new generation of politicians without ideology or organic partisan militancy in time. In this way we go to society, the main quarry of leaders.

A detail to note is that, during the debates of the Constituent Assembly of 1978-1979, the legislators decided, in their eagerness to democratize the political system, until then limited to the majority population of Peru; include the illiterate so they can choose and be chosen. In this last case, the Legislative to proof the social reality and overcome the capture of the State by the elites of the moment. With the collapse of the party system in the late eighties, the parliamentary function began to decline to the point that the parliamentarian transferred its decision-making power to the management of its advisers (with some exceptions), who will end up in practice legislating, as will happen in some future government administrations.

CHAPTER SIX

The new order

I. THE 1993 CONSTITUTION AND THE NEW AUTHORITARY ORDER

In 1990, the general elections were called, and the Peruvian suitor sought new political references in society, being among the closest alternatives: The Democratic Front led by Mario Vargas Llosa and Alberto Fujimori Fujimori with his group Cambio 90. Once again constitutionalism was put to test in the elections. The gravitating themes of the campaign were reduced to the reorganization of the economy and the recovery of peace, aggravated by the previous regime. Added to this, the political management in terrorism, where in the MRTA the family of Víctor Polay Campos, its leader, was aprista being its sponsor of confirmation the own president of the Council of Ministers of APRA, Armando Villanueva del Campo. The new regime imposed the style in the cabinets, by integrating politicians from other parties, as well as independents.

It was decided to ask the Congress for the delegation of powers to issue legislative decrees in order to confront this scourge, many of which were annulled, sharpening the relationship between the political powers. A second disagreement with the Parliament consisted in ruling out the Executive's proposal for the approval of the budget law for the year 1992. Circumstance that reminds us of the episode of eighty years ago with Billinghurst.

Preamble that allows us to contemplate that the events unleashed in the autogolpe on April 5 of that year where the President of the Republic, with the support of the military leadership and a majority acceptance of the population, caused an imbalance in the democratic system dissolving in Congress and ordering the closure of the Judiciary, the Constitutional Court, the Public Ministry and regional governments.

This reorganization allowed the centralization of power around the regime for which Decree Law N 25418 was issued, initiating this period with the so-called "Government of Emergency and National Reconstruction". After the Autogolpe, the government issued Decree Law 25475, on May 6, 1992, establishing penalties for terrorist offenses ranging from deprivation of not less than twenty, twenty-five and thirty years, as well as life imprisonment never seen in the legal and criminal records of Peru:

"Both [Andrés Aramburú Menchaca, dean of the Lima Bar Association and Jorge Avendaño Valdez, dean of the Law School of the Catholic University] agreed that, despite the logical assurances that could be given of a life sentence It must not be forgotten that the legal status of pardon and amnesty is in force.

Theoretically, this meant a 180-degree political turn that aggravated the sanction mechanisms to prevent the release of the person most responsible for crimes in the annals of Peruvian history, appealing precisely to these two institutions that remain in Peruvian legislation, allowing being interpreted in their appreciations "(El Comercio, 1992, p. A7)

After the attack on Tarata Street (Miraflores-Lima), the betrayal of the country was redefined politically and legally and through it, the death penalty became a common sanction. To count legitimacy, the regime proposed its referendum referendum for November 22, 1992 within the process of electing the eighty parliamentarians that would make up the Democratic Constituent Congress (CCD).

Closure of the Congress, during the autogolpe on April 5, 1992.
El Comercio Historical Archive

Avendaño Valdez argued that it was contradictory to propose at the same time the convocation to the constituent parliament and approve the death penalty, an aspect that would entail the modification of the 1979 Constitution where the only entity that ratifies treaties versed in human rights was the parliament, not fitting the possibility of submitting a referendum on said topic. Finally, the consultation did not prosper, deriving its discussion in the future drafting of the constitutional text of the current Charter (article 140).

The Government of Emergency and National Reconstruction had to face the reactions of the international community that forced it to restore the constitutional order, which was reflected in the speech before the Organization of American States, indicating that the following months elections would be called for the Legislative Power and to which the drafting of a new Charter would be entrusted. Once again we placed on the agenda the need or not for the establishment of new rules of the game in the face of this abrupt change and if the political powers would abide by them in their entirety. The recovery of the presidential leadership in front of an extreme fiscalizing congress.

The second mission was aimed at creating conditions for economic recovery. The fujischock that withdrew all protectionist measures in the market and was the largest of the usual paquetazos, came the detachment of the large public enterprises, which mostly came from the expropriations and mergers occurred during the Revolutionary Government of the Armed Forces, several which had been considered strategic and were no longer in the opinion of the state technocrats of the time.

The call for elections allowed the appreciation of political forces defined and recreated for the occasion where politicians who previously supported Vargas Llosa leaned towards the Fujimorist environment, represented by Cambio 90 - Nueva Mayoría that integrated new figures in politics. The new scenario obliged to redesign the Executive-Legislative relations that had given rise to the crisis. For Javier Valle Riestra:

"... parliamentary rationalism was found in unicameralism ... and bicameralism has meant genuflection" (Valle Riestra, 1992, p.14).

"While César Landa argued that: the bicameral system suffers from certain inconveniences that can be overcome by a unicameral system" (Landa, 1989, p. 65).

In the end, the legislators would be inclined towards a one-chamber congress, under the belief that security in the elaboration protocol of the norm with the participation of a group of congressional advisers would replace the second chamber. What in theory was reasonable, in fact led to assess whether these experts qualified to be, especially if they were not appointed from Parliament but recommended by the congressman himself without stating that they qualified for the position. Circumstance that would generate from ghost counselors to upstarts. In practice, this option has not proven to overcome the questions expressed, hence the return to bicamerality does not present any obstacle, in my opinion.

Regarding the rights, it can be stated an extension in those of an express nature but also a restriction with those of an employment nature, replacing the stability section with the protection against arbitrary dismissal.

The creation of the Defensoria del Pueblo (Ombudsman's Office) strengthened constitutionalism by offering the citizen an entity that guides it in the best development of their rights. Promoted by the legislators Carlos Ferrero Costa, César Fernández Arce and Lourdes Flores Nano, the same that was approved on April 12, 1993 and was reflected in articles 161 and 162 of the current Constitution. We must not forget to mention the role played by human rights groups, exerting pressure to make this institution appear in the new Constitution and later to make its implementation a reality that will take three years until Congress elects Dr. Jorge Santisteban de Noriega as Ombudsman of the town. It corresponds to the Ombudsman, that is, to the institution, to protect the constitutional rights of the person, to supervise the fulfillment of the duties of the state administration and the provision of public services to the citizens.

The fundamental right to citizen participation has also influenced the strengthening of constitutionalism, taking as reference the Colombian Constitution, the consultation mechanisms were incorporated as a recall, removal and referendum, whose progress had been established since 1990, but in environmental matters:

"Legislative Decree 611, of September 7, 1990, or the Environment and Natural Resources Code, which indicated the following preliminary provision:

Preliminary Title, Article VI:

Everyone has the right to participate in the definition of the policy and in the adoption of national, regional and local measures related to the environment and natural resources. Similarly, to be informed of the measures or activities that may directly or indirectly affect the health of people or the integrity of the environment and natural resources. All are obliged to provide the authorities with the information they require in the exercise of their powers to control and monitor the environment. "

Instruments that would rethink the political system that until now was only representative and now ventured into the direct attention of the electorate, which must always be instructed so that the consultations are effective and with the supervision and guarantee of the State so that they can be carried out without any mishap. Participation that has also influenced the formation of the National Council of Magistrates, by incorporating representatives of non-lawyers' professional associations to appoint, ratify and dismiss judges and prosecutors. In fact, participation as such has not given the expected result to be some advisers involved in scandals, not missing one that had conflicts of interest and yet remained in office.

In the cultural sphere, legislators chose to redesign the participation of communities in accordance with Convention No. 169 of the International Labor Organization (ILO): Convention on Indigenous and Tibal People in Independent

Countries, which became a treaty of a character binding in relation to indigenous legislation with the ratification of the Peruvian Congress. With him the ethnocentric and monist model supported by the republican constitutions was rejected, postulating one of pluralistic constitutional character, that started from the recognition of the indigenous like different subject but articulated with a State that had to protect it, which demanded the reformulation of what until then it had been the main pillar of the legal organization. To this is added the compatibility in the ways of internal regulation of the right with the validity of human rights to both sexes, as well as the creation of their protection mechanisms.

Circumstance that in its application proposes a more fluid access to the State in the different levels of political representation, in the government and in the administration of justice. Within the territory, if we recognize that the indigenous people enjoy a space, this would lead to a rethinking of the way in which the exploitation of resources through sustained development takes place in practice. From there, it has urged in recent years the need to request an environmental impact report, to determine the possibility of habitat deterioration during exploitation

Territory where the existence of these resources converges with the knowledge available to them, and which constitutes, for example, a very attractive element for some non-governmental organizations and researchers working in rural areas such as the Peruvian Amazon and who then register the species as his, when finally, it is of nature itself. Added to this are the oil and mining concessions granted by the Peruvian government in different regimes and if they benefit the nearby residents, which has been tried to improve with the granting of money from canon rights.

II. THE CHALLENGE OF LEGAL PLURALISM IN THE CONSTITUTIONAL DEMOCRATIC STATE

The 1979 Charter established the course, recognizing diversity through cultural heritage. Subsequently, the legislators resumed in the Constitutional Democratic Congress the need to adjudicate jurisdictional functions to the authorities of indigenous / peasant peoples and communities, within their territorial scope, and following their own customary law - and not the state one - by addressing the creation of the bases of an internal legal pluralism that was limited only by human rights.

This would lead to the conclusion that the work of the administration of justice would correspond to the peasant community (previously indigenous), however, the law 27908 of January 6, 2003, in its article 7, has chosen to assign such work to the peasant round, civil organization created in 1977 and which played a leading role in the fight against terrorism unleashed by the Shining Path and the Tupac Amaru Revolutionary Movement over the past 30 years. We believe that it should be the community, which, through its administrative bodies, should continue to resolve conflicts, as it has been doing.

The adaptation process has confronted two sectors of the doctrine: Those that assumed the position of the absorption of indigenous right to the national normative system and that would probably end up being legislated through a regulation. And the other position that would be that the principle of pluriculturalidad, derived from human rights, end up locating this customary matter and then at the constitutional level.

The constitutional legal pluralism is gradually laying the groundwork for a new order by putting into practice the formal provisions: enforceable, judgments or rules with the so-called alternative non-indigenous systems, which contemplated the resolution of conflicts, all within a process that questions the legalistic legal tradition, related to the slowness of the bureaucratic processes and the presumed inefficiency of the national administration to meet the demands of the common individual. Although pluralism (linked to the customs of the indigenous sector) and the alternative resolution of conflicts - applied to any subject through conciliation - are often related as synonyms, both differ as much for the subject involved as the matter put into question.

The administration of justice in rural areas occurs through the Peasant Communities, whose presidents have the powers corresponding to those of the justice of the peace. The use of common sense and the reasoning derived from customary practices end up perfecting the expression of expressed will. Thus, it is not strange that as a conclusion of the process, the justice of the peace will rule on matters of civil, criminal and procedural law at the same time, which in the formal procedure would be contemplated separately.

Experience that illustrates the role of law in the face of conflict of interests, typical of a society, but where a degree of effectiveness and efficiency in the resolution of conflicts is also perceived and where we can affirm that social anomy would not be generated in formal law ends away from the legal aspect, perceived for example in urban areas in cases of lynching. It can be argued that there is a reintegrating sanction but that it does not dissociate the individual, whose contribution to the community is necessary. The Peasant Communities express a principle of territoriality where the integration of its inhabitants is perceived, who habitually put into practice their customary law, obligatory if there is a consent in between, making it transmissible from generation to generation and where its non-compliance gives rise to to a penalty.

The recognition of the incipient indigenous community autonomy also shows us the existence of its jurisdiction, declaring its faculties and imparting justice. Faculty that would seek a form of compatibility or coordination between the State and those communities (including the rounds), but that is the domain of the state entity, so the proposal of legal plurality should start from there, which does not exclude other ways of approach is through society or the same state authority, but through a concertation. To this would be added the distinction of the administrative levels, typical of a legal-political organization, which would be in accordance with the judicial instances, as well as their areas of competence. Experience that had already been carried out since 1973 and was concluded by the legislators five years later.

"Thus, the legal customs remain in force as long as they are not contradicted. He or those responsible are summoned by the Communal Assembly in accordance with the customary norms, possibly indicated in the statute. But as Pier Paolo Marzo indicates: "When the peasant organization considers that the characteristics of the crime prosecuted does not allow its processing by the community institutions (for example, in the cases of assailants of gangways), they deliver the delinquents to the police authorities or common judicial "(Defensoria del Pueblo 2006, page 19)

But what happens when the assailants are from the community itself or from the campesino round? It would not be strange that they were judged by their own entity, as a kind of law or personal right and that they did not communicate what happened to the official authority. Budget that leads us to distinguish that although indigenous communities have their own normative system to regulate their social life among their members, the conflict arises when dealing with problems outside the community and the legal system, which has a set of norms with different valuations of the same facts. Circumstance that leads us to reflect on the application of law in our country, under incipient integration from the Constitution where indigenous customary coexist and the national legal order that establishes the exercise of jurisdictional functions.

According to the Constitution of 1993, in the last decade we can see the advances in the cultural aspect with the campaigns against illiteracy by transferring the educational policy of the central government to the regions (2010), the publication of copies of the Constitution in Quechua version , Aymara, Ashanika on the part of the Congress; the declaration of sentences in the Quechua language (2015) and in Aymara (2015) through the Judiciary and the establishment of radio and television programs in open signal in Quechua and Aymara (2017), by the Ministry of Culture.

Recently, the Defensoria del Pueblo (Ombudsman's Office) published an exhaustive work in the Attachment Report No. 002-2018-DP / AMASPPI / PPI "The long road to the titling of rural and native communities" that shows the interest of state actors in reducing the pressure of social conflicts in force in the country. To this we add the intervention of the International Institute of Law and Society, among other entities, to mediate and propose a more institutional application of pluralism expressed in the Constitution.

We propose that, under this model, a society be considered developed should be propitiated a very strong impulse in education that leads to the promotion of science, innovation and technology. That it expresses an adequate level in

Human Development Indexes (HDI) that reflects the continuous interaction of the State, present and efficient throughout the national territory. A development that will ensure a level of investment in the human being and the family, strengthening the health system and allowing the opportunity of life projects, either in individual and collective activities, in search of the best conditions.

Under a legal and educational approach, the Constitutional History in Peru can not fail to promote the application of the postulates of the theory of sustainable development enshrined in the Constitution from the Brundtland report (1989). Systematizing them with the treaties and internal rules, which are not only summarized in the protection laws, but showing the existence of emblematic cases that contrast with the need to address the environmental issue as a fundamental right, whose protection must have a perennial concurrence of the State and society.

Finally, it is necessary to highlight the involvement of the different social sectors in the progress of the State, where formal entrepreneurship is necessary, sharing roles in the design and execution of environmental policies. Therefore, informality must be transformed into a positive externality in this process of analysis of exploitation and preservation of natural resources through the Constitution and the law. It is urgent to commit the State (local, regional or national), legal expression of the country and the future National Authority of the Amazon, elected by the members of the different ethnic groups and recognized by the President of the Republic, as Head of State to set the model of development within an economy that does not detach itself from the modus based on its roots, maintaining the quality of life of the inhabitants. To this, we must add the need to continue with the management of the cadastral map, promoted by the Ombudsman's Office (2018), thus avoiding the usurpation of ancestral lands, claimed by the locals. The continuous advice of professionals from different areas would be useful, whose effort would result in banishing any practice contrary to the common good of the inhabitants.

To this we add the need to strengthen the monitoring of the exploitation of resources in those places where formal authority does not exist. History teaches the extensive spoils of which Peru has been victim, being later regularized with bordering treaties.

The lack of enforceability of the State in the responsibility for incidental environmental damage or not is regrettable. Companies that despite being sanctioned administratively, seek the protection of lawyers and judges to continue operating, as at present. Causing with this, the distrust of the villager against the effectiveness of the judicial system in their demands, thus sharpening relationships to become social conflicts, becoming a breeding ground for future clashes against the police. In recent months, indigenous communities and federations FEDIQUEP, FECONACOR, OPIKAFPE and ACODECOSPAT have demanded that the State take immediate measures to stop environmental liabilities, which it has not guaranteed, contributing to favoring impunity.

In recent years, the leaders of the ethnic groups, mainly Amazonian, have realized the potential of raising their claims through social networks and supranational instances because of the way Peru has acted since 2009.

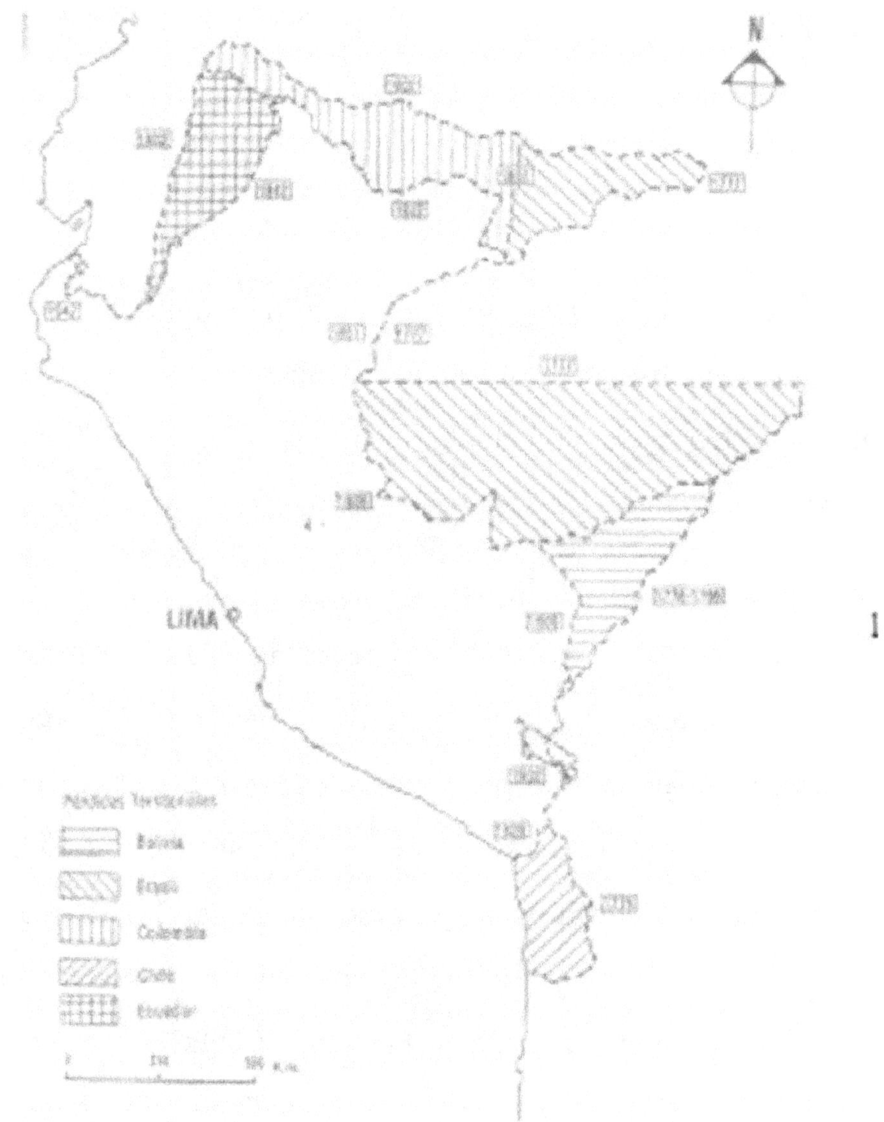

Demarcation and territorial cession Peruvian (1985).

Source: PEASE GARCÍA IRIGOYEN, F. (1985) PERU HOMBRE E HISTORIA. Lima. Banco Continental.

III. OF THE TRANSITION UNCONSCIOUS TO DEMOCRACY SINCE 1993

Alberto Fujimori Fujimori's permanence in power led him to ignore the Constitution he had promulgated, with the backing of the Congress and the real forces, especially economic ones. The persistence of the re-election led the legislators of his party, who they would have more than 50% of the full Congress to establish a Parliamentary Dictatorship that would issue a law justifying the third term, sanctioning any institution that opposed it. Thus, we explain the defenestration of the Constitutional Court magistrates who dared to speak against: Manuel Aguirre Roca, Guillermo Rey Terry and Delia Revoredo Marsano under the accusation of Enrique Chirinos Soto, emulating the phrase of John Locke: Congress can do everything. The constitutional rules were broken again only on this occasion the relations with the supranational bodies, derived from the Pact of San José, were affected.

The election for the third term created the conditions for society to repeatedly press for the end of the regime. The press would be responsible for denouncing the scandals of those close to the government, as well as the presentation of videos that would sharpen the fragility of the system and unleash the resignation of President Alberto Fujimori Fujimori, the succession of power that would determine the appointment of Congressman Valentín Paniagua Corazao as Republic President. Case that is not entirely anomalous since before the collegiate did it since the Constitution of 1823.

We can notice that since then the regimes have been moving successively in the midst of the swings: Alejandro Toledo Manrique (2001-2006), Alan García Pérez (2006-2011), Ollanta Humala Tasso (2011-2016), Pedro Pablo Kuczynski (2016-2018) and Martín Vizcarra Cornejo (2018-2021); sign of continuity, balos parameters that the Charter itself and the constitutional tradition foresee. The validity of the Constitution has been changing according to the political forces that arrived at the political power.

The presidential and congressional elections of 2016 gave Pedro Pablo Kuczynski of the Peruanos Por el Kambio group as president of the republic, while 73 seats of the Legislative Power were captured by the Popular Force party, of Fujimorist character. Circumstance that showed that the political powers had a tense relationship and where an issue foreign to them could be capitalized according to their interests. The members of the Aprista party, since then, have supported the cause.

This is where the present case is located, led by magistrates Manuel Miranda, Marianella Ledesma, Eloy Espinoza-Saldaña and Carlos Ramos, who resumed the classification of crimes against humanity, assigning it to the unveiling of the El Frontón criminal insurrection, which occurred in the June 1986, during the first term of Garcia Perez With this, they left without effect the end of the resolution that declared null the opening order that declared that the facts of the criminal process constitute crimes against humanity ... (Exp. 01969-2011-PH / TC Lima, Humberto Bocanegra Chávez, June 14, 2013).

Circumstance that motivated eleven personnel of the Navy of Peru to accuse constitutionally said magistrates of the Constitutional Court for violating the principle of immutability of res judicata. The subcommission of constitutional accusations again in charge of the Fujimorist party and led by Congressman César Segura raised the dismissal of Judge Espinosa-Saldaña, the suspension of Judges Ledesma and Ramos and the exoneration of Manuel Miranda. In a preventive manner, the aforementioned TC members filed with the Inter-American Court a request for provisional protective measures against their possible dismissal. (Order of the Inter-American Court of Human Rights, February 8, 2018) Provisional measures regarding Peru. Durand and Ugarte vs. Case Peru. (www.corteidh.or.cr/docs/medidas/durand_se_02.pdf)

A fact that illustrates the increasingly recurrent practice of resorting to international bodies, which at the beginning showed the demands of nationals against the State, now it is the state actors themselves who seek in a third party the spirit and the weight required as an authority.

In the current presidential and congressional period there has been interest in reforming the Constitution to reinsert the Upper House, whose presence would not only guarantee the balance in functional parliamentary control but also that of its own members. In this regard, the diplomat Hubert Wieland (2017) in his article: Bicamerality: a Chinese story? proposes reflections on this debate:

"Ultimately, the prestige of the Congress of the Republic will always depend on the moral and intellectual quality of its members and the political will of the political parties to promote the common good not their own benefit" (paragraph 31).

For its part, the Constitution and Regulation Committee chaired by Congressman Miguel Torres has received several reform projects for the Congress, among them the Executive Power Bill 1325/2016-PE, of June 22, 2017, proposing that the current 130 congressmen become 100 deputies and 30 senators, which in my opinion does not respond to expectations by not considering the representation with the increase in the electoral population or consider and the current decentralization model prevailing since 2002.

The Charter has been modified at the regional and municipal level, where the Congress opted to modify the electoral process for mayors and regional presidents or governors, preventing their immediate re-election from the 2018 elections, through Law No. 30305, of March 15 of 2015, which affected respectively Articles 191°, 194° and 203° of the Charter; driven by the scourge of corruption. As for the Congress, since November of 2005, the collection of signatures was promoted in the Moquegua region with the purpose of avoiding the immediate reelection of the congressmen. For its part, the 2006-2011 government plan of the Peruvian Nationalist Party in the field of state reform contemplated the prohibition of immediate presidential, parliamentary, council and regional reelection, under the argument that for the same reason, the same right

This approach made reflect on the parties that had to examine the past of the political candidate, his career, the fulfillment of his promise as his probable aspiration to the next electoral process, which did not escape the existence of certain clientelism with the majority population that being a citizen lacked basic services. Circumstance that put the strategies of the other political parties to the test in the 2006 race, motivating the redesign of the lists, as was the case of Unidad Nacional and Perú Posible, which moved candidates from the list of the National Congress to the Andean Parliament, or they removed them. Occasion that highlighted gaps in the Law of Political Parties:

"Article 24º.- Modalities of election of candidates.

It is up to the highest body of the political party to decide the modality of election of the candidates referred to in the previous article. To this end, at least four fifths of the total number of candidates for Congress, Regional Councilors or Regidores, must be elected under any of the following modalities: a) Elections with universal, free, voluntary, equal, direct and secret vote of affiliates and unaffiliated citizens. b) Elections with universal, free, equal, voluntary, direct and secret vote of the affiliates. c) Elections through party bodies, as provided in the Statute [...] ".

This situation caused other political forces, such as the Peruvian Aprista Party, to adopt a mixed stance where the list of candidates for the Congress was composed of congressmen going to re-election as new candidates, as the law did not forbid it. On March 9, 2015, Congress issued Law 30305 (March 9, 2015) that established no immediate reelection for positions at the municipal and regional level. Provision applied since the elections of 2018, with which only the congressional office continued with the immediate re-election, still.

The President of the Republic, Martín Vizcarra, in his Message to the Nation of July 28, 2018, raised the need to extend the prohibition of immediate re-election to the congressmen, a legislative initiative that was submitted to the Congress for its approval. the measure was not to the liking of this power, made up of the majority Popular Force party, which sought to delay the procedures and discussions. However, when the government indicated that this initiative, like others, was raised as a matter of trust, and given the strong pressure from the community, the plenary session of the Congress finally approved it and converted it into a norm on October 4, 2018.

The law was submitted to a referendum on December 9, and its result was published by the National Elections Panel on January 8, 2019, with which the majority of citizens ratified the presidential measure. Circumstances that warns the protagonism of the president of the republic, under the modality of prior consultation, making the population interested in the march of the State.

Context that encourages us to formulate proposals in order to strengthen Peruvian constitutionalism for future processes:

"First: Faced with the tendency in Peru that the different political offices (mayor, alderman, regional governor, regional councilor, president of the republic and vice president of the republic) are reelected, but leaving a period, we propose that the current position of congressman (later deputy or senator) does not have immediate reelection.

Second: In a similar way in front of other political positions, the one of congressman, deputy or senator will be also renounced, but with the previous approval of the plenary session of the Congress.

Third: The Legislative Power resides in the Congress of the Republic, which is composed of the Chamber of Deputies and the Chamber of Senators.

The number of congressmen is one hundred and fifty-five, made up of one hundred and thirty-five deputies and twenty-five senators (representative for each region). The members of the Congress of the Republic are elected for a period of six years, through an electoral process organized according to law.

To be elected deputy is required to be Peruvian by birth, 25 years and enjoy the right to vote. While, for senator, the same requirements, counting on 40 years.

The congress will be elected by half, every 6 years. Transitorily in the next general election process, citizens through electronic voting will elect 65 of the current congressmen, who will be extended one more year the mandate to become deputies. In that same electoral act, the 25 senators will be elected. The next 65 deputies will be elected the following year.

Fourth: Parliamentary immunities are eliminated. Henceforth, the accusations filed against the political acts of the parliamentarians will be seen in the Constitutional Chamber of the Supreme Court.

Fifth: The budget of the Legislative Power (including deputies and senators) shall not be less than two percent of the budget of current expenses for the Central Government.

Sixth: The congressional function today requires not only popularity but also knowledge, experience and conduct before society and that are accredited by the exercise of their trade or profession, the payment of their taxes. of not having pending or enforceable sentence, counting on the right of suffrage. Which is verified through the corresponding institutions. Who occupies the congressional office (congressman, deputy or senator) at the time this clause is approved and incurs in the causes of non-compliance, will be vacated immediately.

Seventh: The Peruvian regime is republican, representative, decentralized and participatory. Therefore, henceforth everyone who occupies a congressional office (congressman, deputy or senator) can not exercise at the same time in any of the government levels (national, regional, provincial or council) or in the Judicial, otherwise it will be vacated. The figure of the congressman-minister of State disappears. Likewise, if you are an entrepreneur, owner or shareholder, your company can not negotiate directly or indirectly with the State.

Eighth: Each deputy or senator will annually show evidence of its production through the approval of 2 annual bills in plenary, as well as the presentation of a report on the follow-up of the execution of 5 congressional standards, concluding with the implementation for its validity or the repeal of these. Report that will be published in the official newspaper El Peruano, at the end of each term, being the board of directors of the congress, the one in charge of supervising its fulfillment, otherwise it will inform the plenary for the suspension of payment of the congressman for thirty days ". (Gálvez, 2018)

Epilogue: The bicentennial, an opportunity

We can not raise the constitutional parameters without referring to the immediate contexts, in a way that represents their reflection. Paraphrasing Víctor Andrés Belaunde I dare to maintain that even today Peru is still a laboratory test, whose independent life began on July 28, 1821 with roots in the ancestral reality, not always valued and that is currently claimed with legal pluralism, welcomed since 1979.

With the times, we have been changing the discussion of priority issues to find the desired stability. First, the concern in defining the system of government (monarchy or republic), later the congress (unicameral, bicameral or tricameral), the organization of the territory (unitary or federal), later integrating or not integrating blocks (the Federation of the Andes or the meeting as Bolivia, was under the version of Luna Pizarro or Andrés de Santa Cruz), the strengthening of the Congress and the corresponding weakness of the Executive or vice versa, the opening or not to a greater citizen base, the establishment of the internal regulations of the Legislature that would determine the parliamentary control of the representative forum par excellence.

In Peru this connotation in fact rested in the formation of a representative body corresponding to the different political demarcations, before intendencia and then departmental or regional. The legislators, in principle, were part of an electoral minority that could only respond to the requirements stipulated in the political Letters to occupy the positions of Deputies and Senators. This shows us the survival of Hispanic backwardness because parliamentarians were still a reflection of the same society in the first legislatures: Nobles, lawyers, ecclesiastics, military, marine, doctors, merchants, landowners. But as the social composition was recreated from the middle of the 19th century, engineers, university professors, college professors, artisans and in the following century, textile workers, etc., joined its membership. To all this we must mention that the increase of professions or trades developed by men, in the year 1955, the establishment of the right to vote for women made it possible in turn the presence of parliamentarians in the elections of the next legislature.

From the beginning of the republic, by its condition, the actions of the State had more prominence in the political sphere than the legal, hence the objective of the Constitution in the collective mentality was more oriented to state organization and protection of those rights considered as natural -as a response to the fear of excess of power- but not to other aspects of legal regulation in the life of the country. This was not an obstacle to the gradual incorporation of liberalism with norms that demanded the granting of more liberties as well as the creation of new rights for the individual, as long as it favored him by generating his material wealth under the idea of modernity.

Within what we can consider as institutionality-synonymous with governance- we can not fail to mention the expectations of the State since 197 years of republican life the coexistence of the state entity with the presence of the so-called local or regional intermediate powers, belonging to the civilian society whose incarnation was given through the landowners, merchants, the Church, but especially in the caudillo. Important figure for the establishment of new governments.

Its personalism questioned the validity of existing institutions and gave way to militarism as its clearest expression. Since then said phenomenon tried to be controlled from spaces led by civilians and with greater insistence through organized force, first of the associartions and then of the political party with the start of the Electoral Independence Society, which brings together a sector of opinion social in 1871.

The attempts to create an order for the exercise of power determined the production of different constitutional Letters, each of which, in its own way, also proposed the creation or repeal of political institutions such as the Council of State or the Vice Presidencies of the Republic. It also deserves to be noted that some authorities in exercise maintained the existence of an order prior to the fundamental law, as if it were a meta-legal plan and without control mechanisms. Circumstance that potentially endorsed arbitrary practices and subtracted legitimacy from governmental acts. Faced with strong regimes, the episode in history shows us that changes within the state entity were given as rejection to those but not to a structural criterion in the exercise of power.

A relevant aspect that was also the apple of discord was represented in the formation of the different cabinets. Considered and recognized as the right of the President of the Republic; the parliamentary practice determined the almost obligatory suggestion of the president to maintain ministries for members of the Legislative. Situation that translates to an existing preoccupation from the beginnings of the Peruvian State where the Congress did not wish to separate of the Executive, to consider the birth of an entity with its own power; but that years later we can interpret, from the official point of view, as the strategy of both political bodies to give a homogeneous image. Concern about which opposition political parties made use of the congressional body, to demonstrate their interference by fostering a coexistence or, on the contrary, causing a political crisis.

In spite of everything, we can not fail to recognize that the Congress, despite the defects shown in its trajectory part of that fragility of the political system, continues to be the plural representation of society within the State as well as the forum, par excellence, of the debates that concern the institutional life of the country. Maintaining the same spirit of representativeness enjoyed by the congressmen together with the President of the Republic, its vice presidents and the mayors. Political figures chosen for a specific period and who hold a mandate that does not escape that sector of the population that granted their support or electoral preference through their vote. The current Rule of Law represents a great expectation today facing the challenges and to put to the test the institutions that express the will of interest and common good. In this way we can conclude that the account of the events prior to the birth to the Peruvian State allows us to observe recurrent circumstances where the creole leadership has been displaced by the middle sectors, where again the political is disarticulated from the political. We begin new stages of change in our constitutional history, where readjustments in the functioning of political powers are not gradual and, on the contrary, we tend to polarize political forces.

The leader of the leaders has joined the leadership of contentious representation, whose factual leaders have ended up filling the void of an election. We have returned to the policy from the currents of thought as in the nineteenth century, associations today movements, leaving aside the old political parties, effective until the nineties. This episode allows us to argue that Peruvian democracy has been and is a dynamic system, assisted not only by the Constitution and laws, but also by facts and ethics. The circumstances described above suggest that this continuous action has added pluralism, tolerance and an incipient equality of access to information and to the debate that society and the State offer us, promoting the conviction of the elector citizen. Emulating other democratic systems is praiseworthy, but let's not forget our idiosyncrasies without which citizen participation would be catastrophic. It is better to admit what we are to achieve that the institutional reflex is in accordance with the reality that regulates us.

Analysis to be contemplated from the perception of the State from the nineteenth century to the present, where nineteenth-century liberalism proposed that the authority was linked to social representation and endorsed by a new mode of rising character of legitimacy of power where it was stressed the origin in the people, the basis of sovereignty.

Tendency that since 1979 initiated a process of inclusion, but that has not laid the foundations of a formal institutionality, by leaving aside the requirement to be literate to be the ruler and with greater reason the citizenship, giving the opportunity to politicians to tell them half truths Hence, the need for the representative office to recover its temporal or transitory eighteenth-century sense, there being no re-election of any kind. It is urgent to commit the State (local, regional or national), legal expression of the country and the future National Authority of the Amazon, elected by the members of the different ethnic groups and recognized by the President of the Republic, as Head of State to set the model of development within an economy that does not detach itself from the modus based on its roots, maintaining the quality of life of the inhabitants.

To this, we must add the need to support the advocacy work that reduces social conflicts that test the validity of the Constitution. Meanwhile, we can state the use of two political-legal instruments and that are reaching their own development: Go to supranational instances and even to social networks, where people and even state entities raise their claims in a situation of defenselessness, avoiding the abuse of authority despite being limited by the Constitution itself. Second, prior consultation where a group of society or a state power resort to citizens to find support for their claim. A measure that is effective provided that it is known to be used and linked to the work of national representation established since 1822. Today more than ever, the circumstance that the country is going through is constituent. Demand that is not only synthesized in partial adjustments but in a total reform of the Constitution, where political representation, share its leadership with society through political and constitutional mechanisms.

The drafting of a new Charter must come from the concurrence of both the political forces and the consultations to the electoral population, especially in matters of economic regime, limitations to the congressional and public function, the national protection and better control in the informality that unfortunately has turned into manifestations of corruption, attacking the governability of the country.

References and sources

I. DOCUMENTARY SOURCES

Archivo General de la Nación del Perú (AGN)
Archivo del Congreso de la República.
Expediente Nº 01969-2011-PH/TC (Lima). 14 de junio de 2013.
(Caso Humberto Bocanegra Chávez)
http://www.tc.gob.pe/jurisprudencia/2013/01969-2011-HC.html

Ley Nº 28094 o Ley de Partidos Políticos, 1º de noviembre de 2003.

https://oig.cepal.org/sites/default/files/2003_ley28094_per.pdf

Ley Nº 30305 o Ley de reforma de los artículos 191º, 194º y 203º de la Constitución Política del Perú sobre denominación y no reelección inmediata de autoridades de los gobiernos regionales y alcaldes, 9 de marzo de 2015.

https://busquedas.elperuano.pe/normaslegales/ley-de-reforma-de-los-articulos-191-194-y-203-de-la-cons-ley-n-30305-1209275-1/

NEWSPAPERS:

La Abeja Republicana. Edición Facsimilar. PETROPERÚ. Lima. 1980.

El Comercio, 1839-1842; 1850; 1914; 1956; 1958, 1962, 1966, 1967; 1968; 1999.

El Conciliador, 1832.

El Correo Mercantil y Político de Lima, 1822.

El Peruano, 1970-1980.

BIBLIOGRAPHICAL SOURCES:

BAQUIJANO y CARRILLO, J. (1781). ELOGIO al Excelentísimo señor don Agustín de Jáuregui y Aldecoa, Caballero del orden de Santiago, Teniente General de los Ejércitos, Virrey, Gobernador y Capitán General de los Reyes del Perú, Chile, etc.; PRONUNCIADO en el recibimiento, que como a su Vice-

Patrón, le hizo la Real Universidad de San Marcos, el día XXVII de Agosto del año de MDCCLXXXI POR D.D. Joseph Baquíjano y Carrillo, Fiscal Protector Interino de los Naturales del distrito de esta Real Audiencia y Catedrático de Vísperas de Leyes. Reimpreso en el Boletín del Museo Bolivariano (Lima) N.º 12, agosto 1930.

BARRENECHEA, A. (1998). La República Embrujada. Madrid. Editorial Aguilar.

BASADRE G., J. (2000). Historia de la República del Perú. 16 tomos. Santiago de Chile. Talleres de Cochrane S.A.

BASADRE G., J. (1994). PERÚ: Problema y posibilidad. Lima. Fundación M.J. Bustamante de la Fuente.

BELAÚNDE D.C., V. A. (1983). Bolívar y el pensamiento político de la revolución hispanoamericana. Lima. Johm Asociados SRL.

BLANCO, H. (2013): Perú: La reforma agraria.

https://www.servindi.org/actualidad/opinion/365

CÁMARA DE DIPUTADOS:

1849/1850 Actas: Legislatura Extraordinaria.

1912 Diario de Debates. Congreso Extraordinario.

1928 Historia del Parlamento Nacional (Actas de los Congresos desde 1822) Tomo I. Lima. Imprenta Cervantes. Publicación Oficial.

1945 Diario de Debates. Legislatura Ordinaria.

CLAVERO S., B. (1992): Institución Histórica del Derecho. Madrid. Marcial Pons.

COMISIÓN DEL SESQUICENTENARIO DE LA INDEPENDENCIA DEL PERÚ. Colección Documental para la Independencia del Perú (CDIP). Lima.Colegio Militar Leoncio Prado.

(1971) Tomo I. Los Ideólogos. El Plan del Perú. Vol. 5.

(1974) Tomo I. Los Ideólogos. José Faustino Sánchez Carrión. Vol. 9.

(1974) Tomo IV. El Perú en las Cortes de Cádiz. Vol. 1 y 2.

(1972) Tomo XIII: La Obra Gubernativa y Epistolario de San Martín. Vol. 1

(1975) Tomo XIV: La Obra Gubernativa y Epistolario de Bolívar. Vol. 1

(1973) Tomo XV: El Primer Congreso Constituyente. Vol. 1

CONGRESO DE LA REPÚBLICA (2000a) Archivo Digital de la legislación del Perú. Lima.

CORTES GENERALES (1987): Colección de Decretos y Órdenes de las Cortes de Cádiz. Tomo I. Madrid. Publicaciones de las Cortes Generales

COTLER, J. (1978). Clases, Estado y Nación en el Perú. Lima. IEP.

EURÍPIDES: Tragedias II: Los suplicantes. 1995: p. 29. Madrid. Gredos.

DEFENSORIA DEL PUEBLO (2018) El Informe de Adjuntía N° 002-2018-DP/AMASPPI/PPI «El largo camino hacia la titulación de las comunidades campesinas y nativas».

https://www.defensoria.gob.pe/wp-content/uploads/2018/12/Informe-de-Adjuntia-002-2018-DP-AMASPPI-PPI.pdf

GALVEZ, J.F. (21 de enero 2018): Ajustes Constitucionales.

http://blog.pucp.edu.pe/blog/josefranciscogalvez/2018/01/21/ajustes-constitucionales/

GALVEZ, J.F. y GARCIA V., E. (2016). La Historia de la Presidencia del Consejo de Ministros en el Perú. Lima. Presidencia del Consejo de Ministros.

GALVEZ, J. F. (2008). La Historia del Derecho en el Perú. Lima. Fondo Editorial de la Universidad Inca Garcilaso de la Vega.

GÁLVEZ, J. F. (2002). La política como pasión: Breve Historia del Congreso de la República (1822-1968). Lima. Fondo Editorial del Congreso de la República.

GÁLVEZ, J. F. (1999). Juan Pablo Viscardo y Guzmán (1748-1798). El Hombre y su tiempo. Tomo I. Lima. Fondo Editorial del Congreso de la República

GÁLVEZ R., C. (2001), El derecho consuetudinario indígena en la legislación indigenista republicana del siglo XX. En BIRA (Lima). Boletín del Instituto Riva-Agüero. N° 28.

GARCÍA B., D. (2016). Las Constituciones del Perú. Lima. Jurado Nacional de Elecciones. Fondo Editorial.

GRFA, Gobierno Revolucionario de las Fuerzas Armadas (1975). Bases Ideológicas de la Revolución Peruana. Lima. Oficina Central de Información.

GUERRA, F. X. (1996). Identidad et independencia. En: Imaginar la Nación. François Xavier Guerra y Mónica Quijada, Coordinadores. México. Fondo de Cultura Económica.

GUERRA M., M. (1994). Historia General del Perú: La República. Lima. Editorial Brasa. Lima.

HAYA, V. R. (1931). El Discurso de Acho, 31 de agosto de 1931. En: Agenda Perú, Caretas, Pontificia Universidad Católica del Perú. (2002). Los 50 y tantos libros que todo peruano culto debe leer. Lima. Quebecor World.

HERRERA, B. (1929). Escritos y Discursos. Tomo I. Lima. Librería e Imprenta Francesa Científica. Casa Editorial E. Rosay.

INSTITUTO INTERNACIONAL DERECHO Y SOCIEDAD: IIDS BOLETIN. Alertanet. Noviembre 2018. https://mailchi.mp/65515d6bec5d/iids-boletin-diciembre-2018.

JAMANCA V., M. (2015): La Constitución inacabada: Ideas y modelos constitucionales en el momento fundacional del Perú. Primera mitad del siglo XIX. Lima, Centro de producción. Fondo Editorial de la Universidad Nacional Mayor de San Marcos.

JACOBSEN, N. y DOMINGUEZ, N. (2011): Juan Bustamante y los límites del liberalismo en el Altiplano: La rebelión de Huancané (1866-1868). Lima. Asociación de Servicios Educativos Rurales.

LANDA, C. (1989) El proceso de formación contemporáneo del Estado peruano. En: AA.VV. La Constitución, diez años después. Lima, Fundación Friedrich Naumann.

MANRIQUE, N. (2013): Perú: La CIA y el MIR

Texto completo en: https://www.lahaine.org/dT8M

Mc EVOY, C. (1994). Un proyecto nacional en el siglo XIX: Manuel Pardo y su visión del Perú. Lima. Fondo Editorial de la Pontificia Universidad Católica del Perú.

MENENDEZ y PELAYO, M. tr. (1946): Cicerón: Diálogos del Orador. Libro II. Buenos Aires. EMECÉ.

MESIAS, C. (1998). El pensamiento constitucional y la idea de constitución en el Perú del siglo XIX. En: Pensamiento Constitucional (Lima). Vol. 5, número 5. Maestría en Derecho Constitucional. Pontificia Universidad Católica del Perú.

MILLA BATRES, C., editor (1986) Diccionario Histórico y Biográfico del Perú (Siglos XV-XX). Lima. Milla Batres.

MONTEAGUDO, B. (1823). Memoria de los principios políticos que seguí en la administración del Perú y acontecimientos posteriores a mi separación. Santiago de Chile. Reimpreso en Imprenta Nacional.

OFICINA NACIONAL DE PROCESOS ELECTORALES, Centro de Investigación Electoral (ONPE-CIE), 2005. Lima. ONPE.

PACHECO, T., [1851] (1989) Cuestiones Constitucionales. Reimpreso en: IUS et PRAXIS (Lima) Nº14. Universidad de Lima.

PACHECO V., C. (s/f): El peruano frente a la historia del Perú. En: Riva Agüero y Osma, J. de la, V. A. Belaúnde, J. Basadre G.: La identidad nacional (antología). Lima. APD.

PANDO, J.M. de (1998) Manifiesto que presenta a la Nación sobre su conducta pública. En: Pensamiento Constitucional (Lima). Maestría en Derecho Constitucional. Lima.

PANFICHI, A. (2010): La representación contenciosa. La dimensión política de los conflictos sociales en el Perú. En: AULA MAGNA: Crecimiento y Desigualdad: Conflicto y gobernabilidad. Lima. Fondo Editorial de la PUCP.

PAREJA PAZ SOLDÁN, J. (1951) Historia de las Constituciones. Madrid. Ediciones Cultura Hispánica. Madrid.

PAREJA PAZ SOLDÁN, J. (1944) Historia de las Constituciones Nacionales. Lima. Graf. Zenit.

PEASE GARCÍA IRIGOYEN, F. (1985) PERÚ HOMBRE E HISTORIA. Lima. Banco Continental.

PEASE GARCÍA IRIGOYEN, H. y VERME I., Olga (1974) PERÚ: 1968-1973. Cronología Política. Tomo I. Lima. DESCO. Centro de Estudios y Promoción del Desarrollo.

PÉREZ-PRENDES, J.M. (1988). La monarquía indiana y el Estado de Derecho. Madrid. Asociación Francisco López de Gómara.

PERÚ (1989), La Cámara de Diputados del Perú rinde homenaje a la Asamblea Constituyente en el 10° Aniversario de la promulgación de la Constitución política. Lima, 12 de julio de 1989.

PUENTE, J. A. de la (1959) La Emancipación en sus Textos: El Estado del Perú. Tomo I y II. Lima. Instituto Riva-Agüero.

RIVET, P. et CRÉQUI-MONFORT, G. de (1952). Bibliographie des langues aymará et kicua. Vol.I (1810-1875). Paris. Institut d'Ethnologie. Paris.

SAULNIERS, A. H. (1985). Más allá del control gerencial: En enfoque sistemáticos las Empresas Públicas. En: ZUZUNAGA, C. Las Empresas Públicas en el Perú. Lima. Centro Peruano de Investigación Aplicada.

TARAZONA, J. (1946) Demarcación Política del Perú. Recopilación de Leyes y Decretos (1821-1946)- Lima. Librería e Imprenta D. Miranda.

TÁVARA, S. (1951). Historia de los Partidos Políticos. Lima. Editorial Huascarán.

UGARTE DEL PINO, J. V. (1978). Historia de las Constituciones del Perú. Lima. Editorial Andina S.A.

VALLE-RIESTRA y G. O., J. (1992): El fracaso de la Constitución. En: Lecturas Constitucionales N°8. Lima. Comisión Andina de Juristas.

VIDAURRE, M. L. de (1827). Discurso pronunciado por el ciudadano Manuel de Vidaurre. Presidente de la Corte Suprema de Justicia y del Soberano Congreso Nacional de la República del Perú. Lima. Imprenta de la Instrucción Primaria por S. Hurley.

VIDAURRE, M. L. de (1998) Artículos constitucionales que son de agregarse a la Carta para afianzar nuestra libertad política. En: PENSAMIENTO CONSTITUCIONAL. Año III. Nº3.Lima.

VISCARDO y GUZMÁN, J.P. (1959): La Carta a los Españoles Americanos. Lima. Ministerio de Educación Pública.

WIELAND C., H. (17 de marzo de 2018): Los almirantes Petit-Thouars y Stirling en la defensa de Lima en 1881. Recuperado de: https://plumainquieta.lamula.pe/2018/03/17/los-almirantes-petit-thouars-y-stirling-en-la-defensa-de-lima-en-1881/hubert/

WIELAND C., H. (29 de abril de 2017): Bicameralidad ¿cuento chino? La mula.pe.

Recuperado de: https://plumainquieta.lamula.pe/2017/04/29/bicameralidad-cuento-chino/hubert/

WIELAND C., H. (12 de setiembre de 2015): ¿Representan los congresistas a la Nación? La mula.pe. Recuperado de: https://plumainquieta.lamula.pe/2015/09/12/representan-los-congresistas-a-la-nacion/hubert/

About the Author

D. José Francisco Gálvez Montero (Lima, 1960) University of Lima (1991), Professor at the Pontifical Catholic University of Peru (1994), Peruvian University of Applied Sciences (UPC) 2001, San Martin de Porres University of Porres (2003), ESAN (2015) and researcher of the Riva-Agüero Institute (1990).

Doctor in Geography and History (1996). Complutense University of Madrid. Area: History of Law. Lawyer (1995) and historian (1990), by the Pontifical Catholic University of Peru. Specialist in Constitutional Law and History of Peruvian Law.

2018. Award for academic excellence Peruvian University of Applied Sciences (UPC); 2017 Teacher recognition. San Martin de Porres University (USMP); 2016. Award for academic researcher Pontifical Catholic University of Peru.

www.ingramcontent.com/pod-product-compliance
Lightning Source LLC
Chambersburg PA
CBHW080956170526
45158CB00010B/2821